JAN CISEK & SUSAN NORMAN

SPEED READING FASTER

MAXIMIZE YOUR SUCCESS IN BUSINESS & STUDY

WATKINS

Speed Reading Faster
Jan Cisek & Susan Norman

First published in the UK and USA in 2025 by
Watkins, an imprint of Watkins Media Limited
Unit 11, Shepperton House, 83–89 Shepperton Road
London N1 3DF

enquiries@watkinspublishing.com

Commissioning Editor: Etan Ilfeld
Project Editor: Brittany Willis
Head of Design: Karen Smith
Design Concept: Alice Claire Coleman
Typesetting: Andrew Chapman, Prepare to Publish
Production: Uzma Taj

A CIP record for this book is available from the British Library

ISBN: 978-1-78678-922-8 (Paperback)
ISBN: 978-1-78678-923-5 (eBook)

10 9 8 7 6 5 4 3 2 1

Printed and bound by CPI Group (UK) Ltd, Croydon, CR0 4YY

www.watkinspublishing.com

To all past, present and future readers, speed readers, bookaholics and Gilles Deleuze, who inspired me to think and write better.

Jan

To my sisters Penny and Carolyn, the best natural speed readers I know (they just call what they do "reading").

Susan

Contents

START HERE: Read This First

This book tells you how to read it. You can use the speed reading techniques right away.

Read the first few pages sequentially, but only read as much as you need to start using the techniques.

- Each technique is explained briefly in "HOW TO" sections; followed by "TO DO" suggestions. "MORE ..." information follows - only read it if or when you need it.
- Read the Principles and Articles when we tell you to. Look for the grey text at the top of these (and other) pages - this tells you their purpose and what to overlook.
- Each technique improves your speed reading, and you can combine them into a flexible approach that you can use on any text.
- There's lots of additional information that will help you improve. We'll look at this once you know the system.
- If you like to work things out for yourself turn straight to the "GO FOR IT" section (p.5). Get started now - you'll pick up more information as you go.

How fast are you reading now?

To find out **your current reading speed**, start with the **Speed Test** (p.146). Do it again once you're using the techniques to see how much faster you are.

1

MORE Introduction
... if you need it

If you have read the previous page you probably don't need this traditional introduction now. You can always come back to it.

Speed reading means getting the information you want from a text as quickly as possible. Many think that means "reading faster", and this book includes techniques to help you do that. In addition, our approach (developed over 25 years working with thousands of students) offers techniques that help you absorb more information much faster. Having the fastest car is a good start, but knowing the short cuts to your goal can be equally important.

Each technique works alone, and the more you combine them, the more effective and efficient your speed reading, and the more flexible you can be using different techniques in different situations. It's OK to read slowly for pleasure, but it's really useful to be able to speed up, to get whatever information you need in the time available.

You don't have to read everything in this book (or most texts). People are different; texts are different. Only read what you need.

Techniques

Each speed reading technique follows the same basic pattern: a name and subtitle, a short summary and/or introduction, a "HOW TO" section with brief instructions and a "TO DO" suggestion for putting the technique into practice - usually within the book itself. This gives you experience with the techniques and helps you get extra information from other parts of the book. The "MORE ... if you need it" section gives additional suggestions or information - you choose if and when to read this.

Other parts of the book

Additional articles tell you more about speed reading, how to remember more of what you read, or how your eyes work, plus the principles underpinning the techniques (which are also useful in other contexts such as business and study). We recommend you skip these sections first off and read them when directed to use the techniques, in the Quizzes for example.

The book has been written sequentially, but we encourage you to read it in whatever way you choose. The Contents and Index help you find things quickly. The Index is combined with a Glossary, where all the speed reading terms are explained.

Grey text near the top of the page indicates what some sections are (Technique, Principle, Summary, Introduction) and when you can skip pages until you need them.

We use the word "text" to mean any digital or print reading material, including books, documents, case studies. We assume you're reading to get information from a text for business or study. Later, we explain how you might approach pleasure reading, and a variety of other texts such as contracts or scientific papers.

You'll find out more as you go. Whatever your purpose in choosing this book, we hope you'll enjoy building your skills as you become a successful speed reader.

GO FOR IT: Speed Read This Book In 20 Minutes

Before you read any suggestions from us, you might like to try speed reading this book in 20 minutes. You may well be able to work out some techniques for yourself.

WHAT TO DO

Quickly flick through the whole book (in any order), looking for any ideas (ideally 6) you think might help you. (We suggest you focus on the Techniques.) Take notes as you go. Set a timer for 20 minutes – and start.

MORE ... if you need it

Have you done it? Well done if you have. We want to validate things you're already doing well and encourage you to try things out. It's quite probable though that you haven't – yet. But please do, at the first opportunity. It will give you an overview of what is involved in speed reading and help you identify information relevant to you. Reading **about** a subject builds your knowledge. But if you want to gain a new skill you actually have to **put it into practice**. (Would reading a book called *Learning to Swim* be enough for you to jump confidently into the deep end of the pool?) If you want to save time, just read through the **Techniques** and follow the TO DO instructions to give yourself practice. (They'll also guide you to additional ideas that might help you.)

If you've "read" this book in 20 minutes ...

... why would you need to spend any more time on it? Maybe you don't. If you've got from this book all you think it has to offer, then well done.

But if you think there might be more techniques you haven't worked out for yourself, other ways of getting more from your reading or remembering more, or you'd like to know how to approach particular types of reading (print vs digital, contracts, novels, textbooks, history, case histories, computer manuals ...), then start with the techniques. If you feel it would be helpful to understand **why** you're doing these exercises and how to apply them to different materials, read the "MORE ..." sections and additional articles.

Remember:

- It's useful to have a range of skills and speeds you can use with any written materials.
- You'll always have the freedom to snuggle up with a good book and savour every word at your own pace. You're now gaining the additional skills of getting information quickly - or reading quickly through the boring bits so you can get to the good stuff. Read at whatever speed is appropriate. Our suggestions are

designed to give you more understanding and help you remember more of what you read.

- If you have more skills to use when you're reading, you have more choices, more enjoyment and ultimately more time to spend as you want. More is good.

We want you to be in control of your reading. It shouldn't be the texts that control you.

EVEN MORE ... if you need it

Below are more detailed instructions for how to go through this (or any) book in 20 minutes.

You need

- this book
- timer
- paper and writing implement to take notes
- no interruptions for 20 minutes

Preparation

Read through all the instructions before you start:

1. **Set your purpose ...**

    which is **"to find 6 ideas in the book you can put into practice straight away"**

    Note that as you find ideas, you can ...

    - notice but overlook anything you already do
    - notice but ignore anything that just isn't you, that you know you'd never actually do

- notice and **jot down 6 ideas** that you think will help you improve your reading and that you can and will put into practice
2. **Get into a good state by ...**
   - breathing in, breathing out and relaxing
   - smiling (just do it – we'll tell you why later)
   - planning what you're about to do (you're going to read through the rest of the instructions and then follow them)
3. **Set your timer for 20 minutes** and press start.

Method
4. **Find ideas and take notes**
   Flick backward and forward through the book, stopping at different pages completely at random – when you stop, look quickly through the page to see if any ideas jump out at you. If they don't, stop randomly at another page. When you see something that looks interesting, read that bit as quickly as possible, just long enough for you to evaluate the idea. If it's something you will put into practice, jot it down and move on quickly to stage 5.
   Note: Don't get sucked into reading more because it looks interesting – you can always come back later.
5. **Repeat stage 4** until you have **6 good suggestions** – or until your timer pings.
6. **Stop** after 20 minutes when the timer pings. That's it. What you've got, you've got.

(If you're still reading all the instructions so far, stop reading, go back to point 3, and begin your 20-minute speed read now.)

Afterwards

7. **Evaluate** how much information you got. One idea? 6? Somewhere in between?

   - Ask yourself: how long would it have taken you to get that much information if you'd read the whole book slowly? (3 hours? More?)

   - If you had read the book that slowly, would you actually have written down ideas you could put into practice immediately? (Be honest here. How many self-help books have you read? How many suggestions did you actually put into practice?)

TIP

While you're learning, always **evaluate** after speed reading. How much more time would it have taken you in the pre-speed reading days to get this much information? What will you do differently next time? What did you learn?

TECHNIQUE

Preview – see the whole thing

SUMMARY Previewing is a quick look through a text to see what it's about before reading in detail. Look to see where to find the information you need. Previewing builds familiarity with a text, making it easier to understand how the details fit together. It takes 2-5 minutes.
Note: Previewing is for texts **from which you want to get information**. For pleasure reading, just look at the blurb.

HOW TO ... preview

- Spend **2-5 minutes**. (Set a timer.)
- Flick backward and forward through the text, looking quickly at pages to see how it's written, what it's about and where to find the information you want.
- Don't get sucked into reading (unless you only need one small bit of information).
- You're looking FOR ...
    - information you need
    - what's missing - information you need to get elsewhere
- **If you realize you do not need this text, stop** and do something else.

TO DO

If you haven't already, preview this book. Decide what information you need as well as how you will read it.

MORE ... if you need it

Different parts of a text - and what to do with them

Follow these suggestions in any order, if relevant:

1. Look at the **front and back covers** for useful information.
2. Flick backward and forward through the text to:
   - see **how it is organized**
   - notice **layout, design, font size, pictures**
   - evaluate **how easily** you can **access information**
3. Look through the **contents** - or quickly at the **title and beginning of each** section.
4. The **introduction** may help you understand what the book is about.
5. Look for **summaries** - often at the beginning or end of the document, chapters or sections.
6. If you need something specific, look it up in the **index** and check its entries. Glance through the index to see which entries have the most references - that's what the text is about.
7. Open the text at random and **read a couple of paragraphs** to evaluate how well it is written - how

easy will it be for you to extract information?

8. **References** and **bibliographies** show how well-researched a text is, or where else to look for information you need – only read it if you need it.

9. For information that goes out of date, check the **publication date.**

10. Look up **jargon in the glossary** (as you need it).

11. **Recommendations** are more relevant for pleasure reading than reading for information.

12. Skip **acknowledgements, dedications, publishing and author(s) information.**

As you preview ...

- Think about what you're going to do with the information you get.
- Do not get drawn into reading – mark interesting bits to look at later.
- Stick to time. With practice, previewing rarely takes more than 2 minutes.

Notice whether the text is ...

- an "article text'" – it's making a single point in different ways
- a "reference text" – something you're going to come back to again and again for different information
- something from which you can get all the information you need in one work session

Other uses for previewing

As well as previewing individual texts, previewing has 2 other uses:

Preview "the pile"

You may have a pile of books, journals or documents you feel you should read. If you do, allocate an hour to clearing it, spending 2-5 minutes previewing each item. Work in 20-minute blocks (with short stretch breaks) making sure you get through at least 4 texts in each block. Aim to sort texts into:

- urgent stuff which will take longer – prioritize these
- texts you can deal with quickly (in under 10 minutes) – deal with these as soon as possible in a separate session
- texts which are no longer useful – file/throw away
- texts you can put on the shelf to read when you need them – flag them with a reminder, such as a Post-it note on the spine or a highlight in a digital text
- pleasure reading – remove from your "work pile" and put in a leisure pile
- anything else? Decide what to do with them.

As soon as possible, go through your "pile" as described above. Work at variable speeds with different types of material. Think about how you might read different types of text differently.

Preview a booklist

At times many people become students – whether that's an official course or researching a new subject when we start a new job or take on new responsibilities. In this case, gather the most promising books on the subject (on Kindle, in a library or in a bookshop) – or all the books on your booklist. Spend 2 hours previewing them, noting whether they are:

- introductions to the subject
- more advanced
- looking specifically at one or two aspects
- texts you want to start with
- texts to read later in detail

"Reading furnishes the mind only with materials for knowledge; it is thinking that makes what we read ours."
John Locke

Big Picture Before Details

When approaching something new, most people find it helpful to understand the big picture before they can make sense of the details - like looking at a whole forest before you look at individual trees. This makes it an important principle behind speed reading.

Previewing a text gives you an idea of what it's about, what its key features are and where you can find the information you need. Reading a text sequentially means looking at all the details in order before you can understand the whole. It's like looking at a building one feature at a time: brick, brick, window, door, lots of bricks ... until eventually you see that the building is a house. That's not what happens in real life - you see the house and only then look at the individual features in detail.

It's easier to do a jigsaw puzzle if you can see the picture on the box. You still need to put the pieces together (look at the details), but the picture makes it easier to recognize how the pieces relate to one another.

Both the big picture and the details are important. You can always zoom in to the details, but it is important to zoom out and check how these details relate to each other to create a whole. Seeing the broader picture can help you prioritize information and find fresh insights.

TECHNIQUE

Purpose – know what you want

SUMMARY Choose a clear purpose before you start. Know precisely what you want to get from the text in the time available. It only takes 30 seconds – usually while you're previewing.

INTRODUCTION You wouldn't have a productive meeting without some idea of the agenda you expect to achieve, and yet people often start reading a book without knowing what they want from it. It is much easier to keep your concentration with a clear purpose in mind. It's also easier to find information – the words seem to jump out at you.

HOW TO ... set a clear purpose

Pleasure or work?
Ask yourself whether you're reading for **pleasure** or **work**. **(Work purposes include study, learning and getting information.)** If you're reading for **pleasure** (p.107), read in whatever way you like.

The rest of this section assumes you are reading to get information from a text for work or study.

What do you want to do with the information you find?
The simplest way to set a purpose is to ask yourself this
question. Aim to get 6 key points in a 20-minute session
(p.5). Examples: *"I want 6 pieces of information for this
essay/that presentation", "I want the key information
from this text to write a short summary for my boss
- 6 points."*

Examples of well-formed purposes
Business: *Identify 6 trends that will impact my business.*
Study: *Find 6 reasons for the start of World War I.*
Personal Development: *Learn 6 techniques to improve
my time management at work.*

Examples of badly-formed purposes
Business: *To be rich.* (Too general - a goal that cannot be
achieved by speed reading one book.)
Study: *To pass my exam.* (You need a more focused goal
for a 20-minute session.)
Personal Development: *To know everything in this book.*
(The worst possible purpose, p.23.)

Default purpose
If you can't find a specific purpose immediately, imagine
you will tell someone about this text. Aim to find
6 interesting or useful things to say about this text.

TO DO

Jot down 9 or 10 texts you have read recently - as varied as possible. Write down the purpose you had at the time (if any) - and the purpose you would have now you've read this chapter. What difference do you think it would have made?

MORE ... if you need it

Have a "search mindset"

If your purpose is to **gather information for work or study**, change your mindset from "reading" to "gathering information" or "search". With digital reading, consider using the "search" facility.

Purpose or text first?

Either ...

a) start with a purpose then find a text which will give you the information you want; or,

b) decide on a purpose for a text you already want to read.

Know what you want

Before you start reading, and while you're previewing (p.10) ask yourself 2 questions:

1. **What am I going to do** with the information I find?

2. What **specific** information do I want to get in the next 20 minutes?

Examples

A book on **redundancy** will be read with different purposes by different people:

- Personal: Someone who is about to be made redundant. Sample purpose: *find 6 points to find out what my rights are.*
- Business: An accountant working out which people to make redundant. Sample purpose: *6 things to consider to save the most money.*
- Study: A student taking an exam including the subject of redundancy. Sample purpose: *6 pieces of information to answer this question about redundancy from a past exam paper.* OR: *An overview of redundancy - 6 points.*

Skimming or scanning?

Every purpose falls into one of the following 2 categories. Choose one to start:

a) **You don't yet know enough about the text**

   ... your purpose is *6 key points to clarify what this text is about.* You will be **skimming** to find the message in the same way you'd flick through a magazine to see what it contains.

b) **You know what you're looking for**

   ... because you've seen this text before, or you know from your preview (p.10) what it contains. **Scan** through the text to look for something specific. Use the text like a dictionary or reference book.

Note: Skimming and scanning are very similar. You might use the contents or index, flick through the text, look at bold text, headings and specific sections of interest. What is different is your purpose: when you're scanning, you're looking for something specific you think is in the text; with skimming, you're trying to find out what the overall text is about.

Make your purpose SMART:

Specific
Measurable
Achievable
Real
Timed (Timely)

It's easier to set this purpose working backward:
Timed: Give yourself 20 minutes: - the optimum time for an adult to concentrate; you can usually find 20 minutes.
Timely: Read it when you need it.
Real: Don't choose randomly - look for what you need. Consider what you're going to **do** with the information.
Achievable: Something you can realistically achieve in the time.
Measurable: Look for a specific number of points - we suggest 6 in 20 minutes. Having a number encourages you to move forward faster.
Specific: Make your purpose clear and contextualized.

EVEN MORE ... if you need it

How do I use my purpose while reading?

Set a timer for 20 minutes and look quickly through your text for 6 bits of information to fulfil your purpose. Each time you find something important, slow down to be clear about the point, make a note, then speed up to look for the next bit of information.

You don't find information while setting your purpose. You spend less than a minute setting your purpose – then you have a 20-minute reading session to find the information.

Purpose or goal?

A purpose is your reason for speed reading this text now in 20 minutes, e.g. *6 key points to answer this practice exam question.*

A goal is your ultimate reason for reading this text: *to pass my exam, to learn Spanish, to get a better job ...* Your ultimate goal cannot be achieved in 20 minutes.

One purpose at one time

Focus on one purpose at one time. Looking for 2 things at once can double the time it takes. It's better to look for your second purpose in a second session (you'll find it faster as you'll be more familiar with the text).

It's quicker to find information if you know:

- **The context in which you're going to use the information:** If you want to find '6 ways of making better decisions' and you choose one situation (at work, **or** at home, **or** in relationships) you will find the information more quickly (your brain only has to think yes/no once, not 2 or 3 times for each situation). Afterwards, a small amount of thought will allow you to apply your findings to other situations.
- **What you want to do with the information:** Are you providing a synopsis to your boss, writing a section of a report, giving a presentation to a client, colleagues or people at an open session where you don't know how much they know? (Who you are giving a presentation to can change the sort of information you need.)

More than one purpose

While reading, you may spot something useful to you that doesn't fulfil your current purpose. Mark the information so you can go back to it, but stay focused on your current purpose for the 20-minute session. (You might just go back for that bit of information at the end or decide on another 20-minute session with a new purpose.) Some texts are rich enough that you'll know from the beginning you'll be going back to it more than once, each time with a different purpose.

The worst purpose

Why is "gather all the information in this text" the worst purpose? Though this seems to be the unexpressed purpose of most people picking up any text, it gives your brain nothing to choose between. Everything is everything - there's nothing you can overlook. If you really want everything, you'll still gather it faster in several 20-minute sessions, each with a different purpose - and you'll quickly learn there are many things you can overlook.

The best purpose is specific enough that you can say "Yes" (this is information I want - pause to jot it down), or "No" (I can move quickly past this).

Comprehension questions

If you're studying a text, comprehension questions can be used as your purpose - read the questions first and look for the answers.

Asking yourself questions

As you read, asking yourself questions is part of having an alert mind - and can provide mini-purposes. If the information you want is there you'll find it more quickly because your brain is prepared. If the answers aren't there, look elsewhere.

Changing your purpose

As you read you may find you have chosen the wrong purpose (the information isn't there, or you realize you need something different). You can decide to find another text to fulfil your purpose or continue with the same text changing your purpose. Restart your 20 minutes for a new purpose.

> *"If you're not sure why you're doing something,*
> *you can never do enough of it."*
> David Allen in *Getting Things Done*

 TECHNIQUE

Read In Meaningful Chunks

SUMMARY Make sure that you're reading in phrases which have meaning, rather than one word at a time. It might be helpful to check it now. (Several other speed reading techniques also help you do this.)

When children learn to read, there are 2 distinct stages:
- learning how to decipher letters and words
- deriving meaning from sentences

The first is taught along with writing letters – teachers usually check that it's happening by asking children to read aloud. Children are then frequently left to work out for themselves how to derive meaning from sentences. Most don't even realize that it's something they can (or can't) do.

If you can already do this well, skim through this section and move on to the next technique.

Slow readers - read - one - word - at - a - time

Slow readers focus on one word at a time as they read (possibly in the mistaken belief that you can only understand words you are focusing on). Reading - one - word - at - a - time - means - that - you - can - lose - track - of - the - meaning ... partly because it gets boring.

Your brain can operate much faster than that and starts thinking of other things at the same time. No wonder people say they find it hard to concentrate - or that they've read a whole page and haven't understood or remembered it.

Reading faster usually results in better comprehension: concentration is better and your brain has more information to use to understand the meaning.

Reading one word at a time slows people down: stopping 8 times in a row takes twice as long as stopping 4 times.

Read in meaningful chunks

One thing most people can change immediately is to take fewer **fixations** (focus their eyes on fewer words) per line and **take in more words, or bigger chunks at one time**. Your eyes can see a lot more than one word at a time, and your brain can interpret whole phrases or sentences - any meaningful collections of words - much better than individual words.

Look at the difference between reading a paragraph divided into random 3-word chunks, versus the same paragraph divided into varied but meaningful chunks (including bigger ones) - which is easier?

3 words	**Meaningful chunks**
It's possible to	It's possible
get speed reading	to get speed reading apps
apps which encourage	which encourage you to read
you to read	more words at a time.
more words at	The problem is that
a time. The	all the ones
problem is that	we've investigated
all the ones	build the chunks numerically:
we've investigated build	1 word, 2 words, 3 words, etc.
the chunks numerically:	This doesn't help you
1 word, 2	understand the text.
words, 3 words,	
etc. This doesn't	
help you understand	
the text.	

If you're not convinced, try reading each example aloud and notice how much more interesting the information is when it's meaningful rather than robotic. In fact, if you ever have to read a text aloud to an audience, reformat it into meaningful chunks (or make a pencil mark at the end of each chunk), and see how much easier it is to read well.

Using pencil marks to work out meaningful chunks for reading aloud is a useful first step while building this new habit. A good second step is to **cast your eyes ahead**

to find your next break. This may slow you down initially (good if you're reading aloud – it gives people more time to understand you), but as soon as it becomes a habit, you'll do this naturally – and fast.

You may find it odd that we're recommending a technique to slow you down in a speed reading book – recording yourself reading aloud, or reading aloud to a trusted friend, is a good way to find out how well you're understanding as you read. There's no point in reading incredibly fast if you don't understand or can't remember what you've read. Getting the basics of understanding right is an important first step for many people.

TO DO ... if you need practice

Practise reading aloud – look forward in the text to find natural breaks at the end of phrases. Notice full stops, colons, commas, dashes, brackets – all places to pause. Chunks won't be the same length, and as you get better, you'll read bigger chunks.

Note: The following article, "While You're Learning", has been divided into meaningful chunks.

This text is divided into meaningful chunks (p.26) with spaces between each chunk. Cast your eyes forward to the end of each chunk and then pause slightly before the next chunk.

While You're Learning

If speed reading is new to you,   then be kind to yourself while you're learning.   Don't start with the hardest books –   the easiest books to start with   are things for personal development,   e.g. ideas for making better decisions,   saving time,   being more assertive, etc.   First of all,   use the material in this book   to help you learn.

The book is written to help you.   Follow the instructions and you'll be speed reading   before you know it.   We're not telling you   how to win speed reading competitions   or how to impress your friends.   We use speed reading   for getting the information we need   as quickly as possible.   In fact, please don't be tempted   to show off to others –   they're just interested in   trying to trick you,   or prove that you can't do it.   When we first learned   to juggle with three balls,   the first thing anyone said was   "Can't you do it with four?"

Learning means doing things differently.   Doing the same thing over and over   and expecting a different outcome   is one definition of insanity. So some of the things we suggest are not going to be what you're used to, and they're not necessarily going to feel comfortable. ... Try this. Fold your arms across your chest, one over the other with one hand tucked in.

Now do it the other way, with the other arm on top and the opposite hand tucked in. Feels odd, doesn't it? Although some people do it one way and some the other, the one you do feels right and comfortable and the other feels wrong.

Learning is a process, not an event. Each time you revisit a subject you learn or consolidate your learning a bit more. You don't need to practise the system, you just need to put it into practice.

The best first step is to change your mindset from a reader (how many books have I read?) to a speed reader (how much information have I got?). Quality, not quantity.

People learn in different ways – some like to be given clear simple instructions (that's how every technique starts), some need precise detailed instructions or need to understand why they're doing something (you'll find this in the MORE section after the simple instructions), and some like to find out for themselves (you can go straight to the 'Go for it' sections on pages 5 and 65).

Once you know you can speed read (once you realize what it is we've been asking you to do), you don't need to stick quite so rigidly to the 'rules'. We sometimes don't. But if you find that you're sliding back into slow-reading ways, you can follow the rules again strictly and you'll soon get back on track.

Thousands of people have learned to speed read with us, but a few managed not to. They were the ones who didn't do what we suggested. We are telling you everything we know about speed reading in the best way we know how. Anyone can learn to speed read.

TIP

Make a habit of actively noticing every time you learn something new. This activates your "Reflective Intelligence" (RI), which Harvard professor David Perkins suggests will stimulate further learning.

Note: Make sure that you've done the "pre-book" Speed Test (p.146) to see how fast you were reading before. If not, do it now using the article on the next page, "How Your Eyes Work".

Later, when you're using all the techniques, do the Speed Test again to compare how quickly you're reading after using this book - do this second test with the "How to Remember" article (p.128). Then use the memory article as the starting point for improving your memory. Your brain loves learning new things.

We suggest you use this article for your first 3-minute speed reading test (p.146). The total word count so far is given at the end of each paragraph. (Don't stop to try things out while you're doing the speed test.) Start your timer and start reading from the title "How Your Eyes Work". You don't need to read this article in order to speed read, but it provides an explanation and validation for some of the techniques we suggest, and you might find it interesting - particularly the final box - when you have time to read it.

How Your Eyes Work (and how they work with your brain)

An optician once told Susan that speed reading was impossible because "eyes can't move that fast". He might have known about eyes, but he clearly didn't understand speed reading, and must have been a pretty slow reader himself if he thought that your eyes have to focus on every word as you read. [53 words]

We think it's worth mentioning a couple of things here about how your eyes and brain interact when you're reading.

You're more likely to do things in a new way if you know why you're doing them. [37 words/total 90]

How your eyes work

There are a couple of things you need to know about how your eyes work – each of which suggests things you can do differently. [28 words/total 118]

Note: Everything written in this section assumes that you have two eyes which work optimally. We know that many people have problems of different kinds with one or both eyes, but since we can't go into all the options, please take account of those things which you can do with whatever kind of vision you have. If you can read, you can also speed read. [65 words/total 183]

Saccades

Although it can feel as if your eyes are moving smoothly along the line as you read, in fact they are making little jumps – known as **saccades**. Each point where your eyes stop is called a **fixation**. [38 words/total 221]

If you want to test this, as you read the next bit of this section, close one eye, touch the eyelid lightly with a finger and continue reading with the other eye. Since the eyes move together, the little jumps your finger feels through the closed eyelid are reflecting the jumps made with the eye which is reading. Your eyes don't like to get too "fixed" in any direction when you're reading. [72 words/total 293]

Foveal and peripheral vision

Only a very small part of what you can see with one or both eyes is totally in focus – the part you are looking at directly, which is where the light is reflected through the lens onto the centre of the retina during a fixation. You don't usually notice this because the brain is able to decipher visual information even if it is not completely in focus. You focus with your **foveal** vision (or your **macular** vision) and anything which is out of focus is in your **peripheral** vision. [93 words/total 386]

Cinematographers can bring this to your attention by focusing the camera lens on something close up which you then see clearly, while the background is blurred, and then switching to something further away, in which case the close-up is blurred and the background is in focus. [46 words/total 432]

You can play with this a little by holding both hands in front of your face with the tips of your index fingers touching. Focus on your fingers and, without moving, notice how much of your other surroundings is in focus to a greater or lesser extent. Then, again without moving, switch your gaze to something on the far side of the room and notice that your fingers become blurred. Move your fingers slightly apart and notice that your fingertips seem to join into a little island between your two hands. This effect is due to both peripheral vision and dominance. [101 words/total 533]

Your brain seems to take more notice of things in peripheral vision (a weak signal) than it does those of things in foveal vision (the things that you think your brain is consciously concentrating on). Speed readers are confident that their brains can pick up much more information in peripheral vision than from concentrating on every word. [57 words/total 590]

Dominance

Just as you probably consider yourself right- or left-handed, so you also have a dominant and a non-dominant eye (and ear, foot and which side of the brain you favour). When you look at something (e.g. a finger) with both eyes, it seems to line up against the background according to where the dominant eye sees it. If both eyes switch to focusing on the background, your brain "sees" the finger according to where each eye sees it and you seem to see 2 fingers. Dominance does not particularly affect speed reading, but it may have affected how easily you learned to read. [104 words/total 694]

Speed reading is partly to do with your eyes, but it is mostly to do with your brain and your thinking. [21 words/total 715]

Aspects of how your brain works

Knowledge about the brain is growing and gets updated all the time. We have found the following information useful for helping us understand how people read and learn differently. [35 words/total 750]

Right/left brain dominance

The outermost part of the brain, the crinkled white part, is called the neocortex, and it is this part which deals with higher thinking. It is divided down the centre, front to back, into two halves, called hemispheres. Various areas of the brain have specific functions, but in general terms, the right hemisphere (often colloquially called "the right brain") and the left hemisphere prioritize different qualities. If you look at these two lists of words, which one better describes you and the way you think? [89 words/total 839]

Logic	Intuition
Likes language	Patterns
Facts (what is)	Hypothesis (what if?)
Numbers	Shapes
Measuring, counting	Imagining
Sequence	Experiment
Control	Spontaneity
Structured	Random
Organized	Disorganized
Individual parts	Whole thing
Objective	Subjective

[30 words/total 869]

If you chose the left column, you might describe yourself as "left-brained", and you probably do quite well academically, as traditional schools and academic institutions play to the strengths of people who are left-brained. If you feel more "right-brained" (words in the right-hand column), you probably think of yourself as artistic. [51 words/total 920]

The word "dominance" is not a fixed term. For some people it can be a very strong preference, and for others it can be a slight inclination. And just as there are people who are ambidextrous (they write as well with their left hand as with their right), there are people who can work equally well with either side of their brain, either because they were born that way or because they have trained themselves to try out different ways of doing things. If you've ever broken the arm or hand on the side you write with, you may well have managed to teach yourself to write with the other hand, for example. [113 words/total 1033]

However, people usually find it easier to use (in the first instance) whatever hand, eye, foot, ear or brain hemisphere is naturally dominant. Forcing someone to use their non-dominant side can cause them unnecessary stress – and stress is one of the biggest barriers to learning and can lead to other problems. (Just to confuse things, it is possible for a person's brain preference to be opposite to the preference of other body parts.) [73 words/total 1106]

The dominance combinations are many and some of them can make reading easier or less easy. In simplified terms, information tends to be noticed first with the dominant eye – and then it has to reach the left side of the brain and the part which processes language. And the other thing to know is that the right side of the brain controls the left side of the body and vice versa. So, being right-eyed and left-brained makes reading easier. [79 words/total 1185]

Other combinations can slow things down as information is passed backward and forward across the brain – and if you are not naturally left-brained, you are having to process language with the part you are less happy to use. None of this means that you can't learn to read. It just might take longer for some people, and it can be disheartening if they see others doing things more quickly than them. [71 words/total 1256]

With a bit of perseverance, these people can build the habit of reading – and they may even read more proficiently than people who have the best dominance profile but just don't put in the practice. Because speed reading encourages the use of peripheral vision and seeing whole chunks of text rather than individual parts, it usually helps everyone read faster and better, and it can make a huge difference for people who have considered reading "hard". [76 words/total 1332]

In summary, none of the dominance combinations stop you from learning to read, and none of them stop you from learning to speed read. But it may help you understand why some things are initially easier for some people than others. And if you've found reading difficult in the past, you may well find that speed reading techniques are exactly what you need to help you read fluently. [68 words/total 1400]

Also, people are different in many different ways. Different things can be easier or harder for different people, so judge your progress against your own starting point – not against others. [30 words/total 1430]

Triune brain

Something useful for understanding learning is the idea of the "triune brain" proposed by Nobel prize-winner Paul MacLean. It states that the order in which the parts of the brain originally evolved were:

1. the reptilian brain, which mainly controls the body's survival systems, such as breathing, digestion, movement, temperature, etc. Its key motivators are "survival and avoiding harm".

2. the limbic system, or "mammalian brain", which is involved in our emotions and in long-term memory. Its key motivator is "seeking pleasure".

3. the neocortex, which is where higher thinking takes place. Its key motivator is "quest for novelty". [101 words/total 1531]

Broadly speaking, information coming into the brain from the senses passes through the brain in this order. So, if you have physical conditions, such as being very hungry or thirsty, or too hot or cold, or any strong emotion (positive or negative), it will make it much harder to think clearly. This means it is a good idea to sort out any physical concerns during breaks and before you settle down to work or learn.

Getting into a good state before you start reading also helps control emotions and focuses attention on work so the neocortex can work optimally. It is not impossible to think if conditions are not ideal, but you have almost certainly had the experience of being unable to concentrate on what someone was saying because you needed to go to the bathroom or were very cold or hungry, or being unable to express yourself clearly because you were feeling a strong emotion (such as attraction to another person, or anger). Since what drives the limbic system is to seek pleasure, it is understandable that it's very difficult to read something for pleasure and information at the same time – the limbic system's preference for pleasure comes before the ability of the neocortex to focus on information and new learning. [212 words/total 1743]

The fun information in the box which follows also shows why it is not necessary for the eyes to focus on every word because of something called "gestalt"; the brain's tendency to put together partial information and see the whole. You may not notice for a long time that someone is missing a finger – you assume (the brain assumes) that each person's body is "complete" unless you specifically notice that it isn't. This tendency works with language too – making it possible to skim over a lot of information and still understand it. [92 words/total 1835]

PARTIAL INFORMATION

It is not necessary for your eyes to see every letter in a word, or even to see every word, for your brain to understand it. Your brain likes to fill in the gaps when there is not enough information. These days most people can easily decipher incomplete or incorrect words because they're used to the many inaccuracies in digital messages. Guessing, or predicting, is an important technique when you're reading. Guessing the meaning of individual words helps build vocabulary. Guessing or predicting what a text is about primes your brain to look for the meaning – even if your prediction is wrong, your brain will notice the correct answer. Good readers do it all the time.

Try the following examples. [122 words/total 1957]

1. Cambridge research

You may hvae cmoe arcsos an olnine txet aoubt porpoesd rsceearh at Cmabrigde Uinervtisy. Tehy are aprapnelty tiryng to porve taht wehn yuor'e raednig, it deosn't mttaer in waht oderr the ltteers in a wrod are, the olny iprmoatnt tinhg is taht the frist and lsat ltteers are in the rghit pclae. The rset can be a ttoal mses and you can sitll raed it wouthit porbelm. The raeosn is taht the bairn deos not mkae snesne of wrods lteter by leettr, but by lokonig at the wrod as a wlohe. The rsceearh deos not esixt, but tihs text shwos taht the ieda is itnreetsnig. [108 words/total 2065]

2. Tops and bottom of letters

If half the letters are covered, you can still get a good idea about what is being said. (It's easier with the tops of letters because they are more varied than the bottoms.) [39 words/total 2104]

Notice how relatively easy it is to read a text where you can only see the tops of letters.

It can be more difficult to understand if you can only see the bottoms of letters.

[35 words/total 2139]

3. Redundancy and predictability

Language includes a lot of redundancy – things are said more than once in different ways, so you might not need to read each example. Language is also often predictable – there are set expressions and grammatical rules which are easy to anticipate. When you've been reading, you've almost certainly turned a page in the middle of a sentence and known what the first word on the next page is going to be. Try predicting what you think the next word after each of these examples will be. (The answers are on p.169 – but if you say something that has the same meaning, or which is similar but not an important concept, then you still have a correct answer.) [121 words/total 2260]

a) I'm looking forward ...

b) A stitch in time ...

c) 21 today? Happy ...

d) On the one hand it tastes good, but ...

e) After trying for years without much ...

f) It was kept secret until 50 years after his ...

g) It was growing bigger and ...

h) After forgetting so many things, we wish we could ...

i) What actually happened, we may never ...

j) Lions, both in zoos and in the ...

[70 words/total 2330]

Except in a few specific circumstances, such as legal documents, it is the meaning that matters, not the specific words. [20 words/total 2350]

TECHNIQUE

Identify Hotspots – know what to overlook

SUMMARY Know what to read and what to overlook – in terms of message and types of words. Hotspots are words which carry the information you want. You're looking **at** words, sentences, paragraphs, etc., but what you're looking **for** is meaning, or the message. Skim quickly past parts which aren't relevant and slow down, zoom in and read more carefully when you find hotspots.

HOW TO ... identify hotspots

Hotspot is a shorthand term for any information you need when reading, either to find **something specific you're looking for**, or to **understand the meaning or message of the text.**

Essentially, what you're looking for is **meaning**. What is the **information, opinion or idea** that the writer is expressing? **Hotspots are the bits of information that you need while you're reading now.**

Keywords are the words which carry the most meaning in a sentence. You need to notice keywords to help you identify which ideas are important to you now (hotspots).

TO DO

This activity will help you understand hotspots. Use the section "Priming" (p.52). Read it at whatever speed you are comfortable with in order to understand the text, and answer the following questions:

1. Which 2 sentences in the first paragraph summarize what priming is?
2. Underline the minimum number of words you need to understand that message.
3. What are all the other words doing?
4. Compare your answers with ours below.

Answers

1. Your **brain** is **primed** to **recognize** something **consciously because** it has **seen** it **before** (even if you haven't consciously noticed it). Your **brain notices much more**, and much more **quickly, than you** can **notice consciously.**
2. See bold text in 1.
3. See "What are the other words doing?" (p.47) to see what words to overlook.

The following information about "Priming" might also help you: the first 2 sentences explain the conscious and non-conscious mind. This is important for (most) people who haven't thought or known about this before. Some people will need to read this information, but if you already know it you can skim past.

The sentence about advertisers is an example of people using this information. It is designed to convince you. Paragraph 2 is a further (practical) example to convince you. You will read one or both of these if you need convincing (if this is a completely new concept for you) – if you accept that the author is telling the truth, you can skim quickly past these 2 examples, and probably think about the paper folding rather than doing it.

Paragraphs 3 & 4 explain how priming is related to speed reading – to help you understand how and why these techniques work, and to boost your confidence. You don't need to read them if you are not interested or if you already know the information.

Keywords

The words which **carry the most meaning** are usually things you can make a mental picture of:

- **nouns** (things), e.g. *brain, building, summer, love, politics*
- **verbs** (action, "doing" words), e.g. *thinking, cooked, strolling, met, makes, driving*
- and sometimes **adjectives and adverbs** (descriptive words), e.g. *consciously, hottest, yellow, sad, slowly, excited*

In the following sentence, the keywords are in bold:
*The **bird** was **sitting** on the **highest branch** of the **tree**.*
If you focus on those words (*bird - sitting - highest branch - tree*), you understand the meaning of the sentence. If you focus on the other words, you don't get any meaning at all: *The, was, on, the, of, the*
Note: Keywords will also help you with taking notes (p.83) and reducing subvocalization (talking to yourself while you're reading p.150).

What are the other words doing?

Look at the words you think you didn't need to understand the message of the "Priming" section. **These are words that you can skim your eyes over** because you don't need to spend any time on them. They will include:

- **repetition** - the same idea repeated again in different words - possibly to convince you (the idea may go against tradition, or not be known to many people) or to help explain a difficult concept.
- **examples** - again to help you understand or to convince you. If you already understand or are convinced, you don't need to dwell on these. You might need to read one example to clarify the meaning, but as soon as you understand the concept, you can move quickly on.
- **"grammar words"**, such as *the, a, at, of, is, was*. These are the most frequent words in the language - and they can be mostly ignored!

Zooming in

You're quickly skimming through pages for the message, or scanning for specific information – and you notice some keywords related to your purpose which help you find a hotspot, a piece of information you need. Now **zoom in** to the text – which means **reading a bit more slowly until you're sure you understand it**. If necessary, make a note of the information (note down keywords, mark it with a Post-it, or record an audio file). Then **speed up again to look for the next hotspot.**

It's OK to slow down for important information, but don't get stuck reading slowly.

How do you "quickly skim past"?

How do you read and not read? You look quickly through the text, get an idea of what it's about and decide immediately whether you need to look at it more closely or not. **As soon as you know it's not what you're looking for, move on.**

You can also overlook lists, tables and diagrams – note what they are about, but you do not need to read them in detail unless you need that particular information immediately (you can always come back to it).

"Watch out" words

Negatives: There are some important "small" words which you can't overlook. We call them "watch out" words (because you must always watch out for them).

They are words such as **not, never, don't**, which give exactly the opposite meaning to a sentence:

> The **bird** was **not sitting** on the **highest branch** of the **tree**.
>
> He never said that he would go.
>
> **Don't** catch the next train.

While you are still learning to focus on the meaning of words, just remind yourself before you start reading that meaning includes **negatives**.

Alternatives: There are also words which indicate that there are 2 (or more) possible points of view: *however, but, alternative, other, on the one hand,* etc. If you miss or misunderstand these words, it usually becomes clear as you read and the subsequent information doesn't make sense. Similarly, a word might lead you astray. The word "bunker" for example could make you think of war, but then you realize the passage is actually about golf. In these situations, go back and check. With experience, though, you will notice those alternatives on first reading, and slow down slightly to make sure you're clear which one the author is promoting.

Also look out for words such as "firstly/in the first place" which may indicate a list of different ideas to take note of, or "in other words" which indicates a repeated explanation of the same idea - only read this if you haven't understood yet.

Chapter titles, bold text, etc.: Whatever you're reading, always look out for **titles, subtitles, text in bold type, boxed information, pull quotes** (words which are pulled out of the text and repeated somewhere obvious in bigger type to attract your attention) and **picture captions**. These words are usually emphasized because they are important.

Keep in mind that the author has to write everything anyone might need - including publishing information, acknowledgements, references, etc. You are not "anyone"; you are you. If you are a beginner you might need to read a lot of the information, but if you already know a lot about this subject, you'll only be looking quickly through for information you don't already have. You may or may not need to follow up some references - if you do, just mark them to do later. Sometimes you just need to know where certain information is so that you can look it up later when you actually need it ("read it when you need it").

"The art of being wise is knowing what to overlook."
William James

SUMMARIES

Look out for summaries - these are always hotspots. Train yourself to notice words that indicate summaries: *"to sum up"*, *"in summary"*, *"in short"*, *"in a nutshell"*, *"briefly"*.

You usually read summaries more slowly than expanded texts because the information is denser - but reading the summary of a whole book in 10 minutes is usually time well spent.

First and last (sometimes called "beginnings and endings"): Summaries usually come at the beginning or ending of sections. The introduction and/or first chapter of a book or document usually sets out the theme or problem - and often tells you where to look for it. (A contents list can also be good for this.) The last chapter often gives solutions and sums up the arguments.

Huge numbers of books have been summarized and are available online (often for free) or in hard copy.

Note: Research has shown that reading summaries instead of full texts leads to enhanced comprehension, improved retention of key information, and more effective recall over time.

Priming

We suggest you use this text while working with the "Hotspots" technique (p.44).

Your conscious mind is the part of your brain you think you are thinking with right now - everything you are consciously aware of around you. However, at the same time as you are thinking about something with your conscious mind, other parts of your brain are taking note of everything else around you. So while you're watching a film, advertisers are happy to pay large sums of money for their product to appear in the background, knowing that many people will notice it (even if not consciously) and later feel it is somehow familiar to them and therefore be more likely to buy it. This familiarizing process is called "priming". Your brain is primed to recognize something consciously because it has seen it before (even if you haven't consciously noticed it). Your brain notices much more, and much more quickly, than you can notice consciously.

When you have noticed something, you will recognize it more quickly when you see it again. Try folding a piece of paper in half, then in half again, again and again. Open out the paper and repeat the process as quickly as you can. It is so much quicker and easier the second time (you can even do it behind your back) because the paper is already creased in the right places. Similarly, once your brain has formed neural links between pieces of information, it is easier for it to follow the same pathway the next time. You can do regular everyday tasks almost without thinking of them consciously at all.

We take advantage of this phenomenon when we're speed reading. When we preview a text, even just by flicking through it a couple of times, we are becoming familiar with it, making it much easier to find information when we are consciously looking for it later. Then, while we're looking consciously for specific information, we are confident that our brains are also noticing other things. These may spontaneously come to mind later when we need them, or we may get a feeling that there's something else we need to check.

This is also why it is quicker and more effective to take a 3-step approach to speed reading:

- preview a text
- work with the text to look for specific information
- rapid read through the whole text looking at every page (p.53)

Once your brain is primed with the first 2 steps, you can very quickly read through the whole text, confident that you will notice things you may not have (consciously) noticed before.

Open Your Peripheral Vision

SUMMARY This section explains how to open your peripheral vision so that your eyes are able to see more and your brain can take in more information at a time.

INTRODUCTION Not everything you read needs to be directly in focus – you can take in information through your peripheral vision. In fact, your brain often takes more notice of information this way (p.34). The more information you can take in peripherally, the more your brain can absorb at one time – both consciously (the part you think you are concentrating on) and unconsciously (the things your brain notices even if you're unaware of it).

Once you know how to do it, it takes less than a minute to open your peripheral vision – after which most people say they read more quickly, with greater clarity and comprehension. The effect usually lasts about 20 minutes – during which you do not need to think about it.

HOW TO ... open your peripheral vision

There are various ways to open your peripheral vision. We suggest you try them all because it will help you get used to what it feels like to have your peripheral vision open, and you'll be able to reach that state more easily.

Use your hands

1. Sit up straight. Put the palms of your hands together in front of your eyes.
2. Look straight ahead, past your hands at something at least a couple of metres away. Your hands should be out of focus. Without moving your eyes, be aware of how far you can see to either side of you.
3. Be aware of both hands at once as you separate them (you're still looking straight ahead without moving your eyes), then move them backward till they're approximately in line with your ears, just beyond where you can see.
4. Wiggle your little fingers and slowly move your hands forward a bit until you can see the movement. (You're still looking straight ahead with both eyes – not looking from side to side.)
5. Smile and feel your eyes soften.
6. Take your hands down and be aware of how much you can see to either side of you.
7. You can now start reading without thinking about peripheral vision.

Without hands

Once you've tried using your hands, you can achieve the same effect without them:

1. Sit up straight and throughout the exercise keep both eyes looking straight ahead at something a couple of metres away.

2. Breathe in, smile as you breathe out and feel your eyes soften.
3. Widen your gaze as if you were trying to see behind both ears at the same time.
4. Be aware of how far you can see to either side – then start reading.

Concentration point

In his 2010 book *The Gift of Dyslexia*, Ron D Davis explains how he had extraordinary success helping children with dyslexia read by focusing on the **concentration point**. Since then the point has been used to help many people (with or without reading difficulties) improve their reading to get information faster with better concentration.

The concentration point is about 30cm (12in) above and behind the top of your head. By focusing your attention on that point your eyes automatically go into peripheral vision. Here's how to do it.

1. Sit up straight, and keep your gaze fixed on a point about 2 metres (6.5 feet) ahead of you. Make your right hand into a loose fist and place it on the top of the middle of your head. Then lift it as high and as far backward as you comfortably can, still in the middle, in line with your nose. Imagine a straight line going from your fist to the point at the back in the middle of the top of your head, through your nose and meeting the ground in front of you at a 45-degree angle.

Experiment a little until you're confident your fist is at a point about 30cm (12in) above and behind the middle of your head. (Looking in a mirror or asking a friend to help can be useful at first.)

2. When you're confident your hand is in the right place, keep both eyes looking straight ahead and your mind focused on the point where your hand is - and slowly take your arm down to your side.

3. Smile as you feel your eyes soften and your peripheral vision open wider.

Alternatives

- Once you have located the concentration point, you might find it easier to focus on something concrete rather than a space. As you sit straight with eyes gazing at a point about 2 metres (6.5 feet) ahead, try focusing on an **orange** in that spot. If you need something bigger, imagine a **melon** above and behind your head - or a brightly-coloured **balloon**.

- Alternatively, sit up straight, close your eyes and focus on your 2 feet. Imagine strings going from each foot to the opposite knee. Focus on your knees. Imagine the strings crossing to each opposite elbow. Focus on the elbows. Then take the string to your heart - take a breath and continue extending the strings to each shoulder. Focus on both shoulders. Then extend the strings to the concentration point above and behind your head. Even with your eyes closed, feel your peripheral vision opening up. Smile as you open your eyes.

Note: Research suggests that **positive emotions** (and smiling) increase the expanse of our peripheral vision, and we see more.

TO DO

If you haven't already tried the ways of opening your peripheral vision by focusing on the concentration point, do it now. Practise in those moments while you're waiting for something or someone.

TIP

When you're reading, hold the book a bit further away from your face - and relax your eyes and your shoulders. If you're hunched over your text, you're probably also relying a lot on foveal vision (the part that's directly in focus). Sitting back puts you in a more relaxed state (p.61) and helps you take in more information through your peripheral vision.

Take Fewer Stops Per Line

If you find it hard to break the habit of reading every word individually, this technique could be a useful stepping stone. If you don't need it, go straight to the next page.

Your eyes do not move smoothly along a line of text; they make small jumps (called saccades) from one place to the next. Since it slows you down to read (or stop at) one word at a time, it makes sense to take fewer stops (or fixations) per line and let your brain pick up meaning in your peripheral vision.

Depending on the length of the line, you can start by making 4 or 5 stops per line, then get quicker by taking 3, and then 2 stops per line. When you get to 1 stop in the middle of the page, you'll be super-reading, see Patterns (p.71).

What do you look at?
As you glance quickly along the line, briefly stop at whole words or spaces between words. In either case, you're picking up the meaning from the surrounding words in your peripheral vision.

Once you've tried these 2 different ways, you'll find you don't need to focus on any particular spot. The important thing is that you get used to reading with fewer stops.

While you're practising, you can guide your eyes by drawing pencil marks down the page.

TO DO

Choose any uninterrupted text from this book or elsewhere.

Open your peripheral vision (p.54), relax and smile.

Choose how many stops you're going to make and draw pencil lines down the page.

Read as quickly as you can, consciously moving your eyes just to stop on the pencil lines.

Note: This technique is different from "Reading in meaningful chunks" (p.25), which is a basic reading technique where you consciously look ahead and read in your mind to understand the meaning.

"Taking fewer stops" is a step on the path to full speed reading. Rather than focusing on specific words, you use your peripheral vision to notice chunks of text from which your brain works out the meaning.

TECHNIQUE

State – feel good

INTRODUCTION The optimal state for reading is relaxed, focused and alert. Having a regular sequence for getting into a good state builds a habit which helps you counteract stress, perform better and take in more information quickly. Getting into a good state takes less than a minute.

HOW TO ... get into a feel good state

- **Breathe in** and relax your body as you breathe out.
- **Open your peripheral vision,** e.g. by directing your attention to your concentration point to help you focus (p.56).
- **Smile** – to feel more positive.
- **Pause and plan** your next speed reading task.

TO DO

Take a moment now to enter the "feel good" state as described above.

Make a habit of getting into this state before speed reading sessions.

MORE ... if you need it

Stress is the cause of a lot of difficulties with reading and learning for many people. A simple sequence can help you release stress – if you already have a sequence of your own, you can use that. The more you do it, the more you can focus on your reading.

You can maintain this state for about 20 minutes as long as there are no interruptions. After that, you can easily repeat the process to stay engaged and productive. Here are some tips on how to maintain concentration for the full 20 minutes:

- **Drink water** on a regular basis to refresh and help maintain optimal body functions. Dehydration negatively impacts brain function, impairing cognition and attention and causing forgetfulness, among other things.
- Have **regular breaks** and stretch occasionally, preferably standing up and moving around. Step outside (or open a window) to oxygenate your brain. According to research, we remember more from the beginnings and endings of work sessions ("primacy and recency effects"), so having more breaks also helps you remember more.
- **Smiling.** Research suggests both physiological and psychological benefits from maintaining positive facial expressions (smiling!) during stress.
- **Sleep** is important because we take in information

more easily when we are alert. It is also crucial for processing and consolidating a day's learning.

Questioning

"Questioning" is an additional element of an optimal state for reading (and learning): **relaxed, happy, alert and questioning.**

Before reading, ask yourself: *"What do I expect to get out of this text?"* Even if your expectation is not met, you'll know it more quickly if you ask this question. If the information is there, you'll find it more quickly.

During reading, ask yourself: *"Is this useful for my purpose?"* This will help you focus and decide what information to take note of.

After reading, ask yourself: *"What did I get? Is there anything else I need?"*

TIP

Getting into a good state is also useful before you give a presentation, go in for an audition, interview or exam, or talk to customers or patients. The more you do it, the more it becomes a habit as your body finds it easier to relax into a good state – and therefore the more effective that state is when you are in a potentially stressful situation.

EYE EXERCISES

It's harder to read when your eyes are tired or strained. Regular eye exercises can prevent eyestrain. Do one or more of these exercises from time to time to keep your eyes fresh for reading:

- **Changing focus:** Every 20 minutes or so, close your eyes briefly, then alternately look at objects nearby and far away, and ensure your eyes adjust focus each time.

- **Palming:** Warm your palms by rubbing them together a few times, close your eyes and gently place your palms over your closed eyes for 30 seconds.

- **Clock gazing:** Sit straight and imagine a large clock face about 30cm (12in) in front of you. Without moving your head, move your eyes up to the 12, and down to the 6, then continue sequentially to 1 then 7, 2 then 8, right to 3, left to 9, down to 4, up to 10, down to 5, and up to 11. Close and rest (or palm) your eyes for a moment afterwards. (You can do this exercise with your eyes closed.)

GO FOR IT: Just Read Faster

This is another opportunity for you to work out speed reading for yourself before reading the entire book.

WHAT TO DO

Just look down each page of this book (or any other text) at about 5 seconds per page and gather as much information/meaning as you can. You may find after a few pages that you're able to understand what the pages are about. Keep going as fast as you can.

MORE instructions ... if you want them

1. Choose any book with uninterrupted text. Start on a full page. Set a timer and start reading "normally" with comprehension. When you get to the bottom of the page, check your timer to see how long you've taken. Write down the time.

2. Now set your timer for half the time you've just spent. Read the next page as fast as you can and stop when the timer pings. You may find it helpful to guide your eyes with your finger moving in a wiggly line down the page. You've only got half the time so do whatever

you have to do to get to the bottom of the page.

Evaluate your progress.

- Did you reach the end?
- Did you try taking fewer stops per line?
- How much have you understood?
- Notice how you had to read a bit differently in order to get to (or somewhere near) the end of the page. Do you know what you did?

3. Repeat step 2 with a new page, setting your timer for THE SAME time as you've just done, making sure you get to the end of the page. Evaluate your progress again. (You're reading twice as fast as you were at the beginning.)

4. Repeat step 2, but halving the time again. Then keep reading at that speed, just understanding what you can, to the end of the article or chapter. Then jot down a few notes about what you've understood.

If you've just worked out what to do for yourself simply by speeding up, then you'll be able to whizz through the rest of this book - there are still quite a few techniques which will help you get the information you need in less time, but you've cracked the question of reading speed.

We've done this with young people - sometimes just saying "Read as fast as you can". Since they're used to doing what the teacher tells them, lots of them have worked it out for themselves too.

Speed Up ... your eyes and your brain

We hope that if you tried "just reading faster" in the previous section, you noticed how it's possible to miss a lot of words and still understand what the text is about - and therefore when to zoom in and slow down to read in more detail. Using this "speed up" technique will allow you to do this even faster.

SUMMARY Speed up your eyes and your brain before you start reading for information. It only takes a minute and the result is that you can read faster - often doubling your speed (or more).

INTRODUCTION This is not a technique for reading - you are not gathering information. The purpose is to speed up your eyes and your brain so that you'll be able to gather information more quickly from anything you read immediately afterwards.

Note: To test how well this technique works, follow the before and after "Speed Test" instructions (p.146) for 1 minute not 3.

HOW TO ... speed up your eyes and your brain

Use the text "How Your Eyes Work" (p.32). When you get to the end of the text, just carry on with the following pages of the book.

1. Get into a good state: breathe in, relax as you breathe out, open your peripheral vision by focusing on your concentration point, smile and pause to think about what you're about to do.

2. Read as you usually do, while at the same time underlining the words you're reading with your finger (as children often do), for about 4 lines, making sure you're reading the words (not looking at your finger).

3. Continue underlining with your finger, but as fast as you can – at about one second per line, without worrying about understanding. Keep focusing on the words above your finger, moving your eyes at the same pace as your finger. Initially you may not even see the words and you should be **going faster than you can understand**. If you can understand the meaning then move your finger and your eyes faster. **Note:** If you slow down now, you won't speed up your eyes and brain enough to get the benefit.

4. Keep going as fast as you can for 2 or 3 pages. After a short while you'll begin to notice words as your eyes fly over them. Do not slow down. Once you have started to see some words as

you go at 1 second per line, continue for about another page.

5. Stop. Now you're ready to read with comprehension.

You can use this speeding up technique with any text. Speed up your eyes and brain with the technique, then go back to the beginning of the text and read as fast as you can with comprehension. (By using this technique you have also primed your brain to understand it more quickly.) This can be a useful way to wake up your brain at the beginning of a reading session.

Note: You can also use the patterns in the next section (p.71) to speed up your eyes and your brain before you start speed reading with understanding.

MORE ... if you need it

Speed is relative. When you set off in the car on a cold morning with ice on the ground, even the slowest speed can feel as if you're out of control. Yet if you've been driving fast along a motorway and then you come off into a residential area, it can be really hard to drive slowly because your brain is still reacting fast. You can use this fact before you start reading to get your brain and eyes working more quickly – and reading faster.

Thin Slicing

If you want to get the best experience of a cake, how would you cut it? (It's not a trick question.) Vertically, right? You'd cut a vertical slice so you could try every part of it. And you'd only need quite a thin slice. And yet most people read a text as if they were eating a cake from top to bottom, layer by layer.

The concept of taking a thin slice from a cake is known as "thin slicing", and it was popularized by Malcolm Gladwell in his book *Blink*. It is one of the key principles underpinning our approach to speed reading. You aim to get the meaning and important details from a text by focusing on these aspects as quickly as possible without reading more than you need to.

As you learn the different techniques, notice how the focus is always how to **get more from less**.

Patterns ... to look for information

INTRODUCTION Try some of the patterns speed readers use when they're looking quickly down a page for hotspots (p.44). The 3 most common patterns are: underlining, super-reading and zigzag. When you've found a hotspot, zoom in to read in more detail, usually using the underlining pattern. Then, go back to using a different pattern to find other hotspots.

HOW TO ... use patterns

Underlining

- If you are reading this book sequentially, you have already experienced underlining (p.68).
- Place your finger under the line of text and read as quickly as you can with your eyes following your finger.
- To speed things up, cut off the beginning and ending of each line. The meaning should still be clear from the words you focus on.

Your conscious mind is the part of your brain you think you are thinking with right now – everything you are consciously aware of around you. However, at the same time as you are thinking about something with your conscious mind, other parts of your brain are taking note of everything else around you. So while you're watching a film, advertisers are happy to pay large sums of money for their product to appear in the background, knowing that many people will notice it (even if not consciously) and therefore feel it is somehow familiar to them and will be more likely to buy it. This is called 'priming'. Your brain is primed to recognise something consciously because it has seen it before (even if you haven't consciously noticed it). Your brain notices much more, and much more quickly, than you can notice consciously.

Super-reading

- Put your finger in the middle of the top line of the page.
- Following your finger, look down the middle of the page, wobbling your finger slightly from side to side as you go.
- Notice the words in the middle and be confident that your brain is picking up information on both sides and will notice the information you're looking for.

Your conscious mind is the part of your brain you think you are thinking with right now – everything you are consciously aware of around you. However, at the same time as you are thinking about something with your conscious mind, other parts of your brain are taking note of everything else around you. So while you're watching a film, advertisers are happy to pay large sums of money for their product to appear in the background, knowing that many people will notice it (even if not consciously) and therefore feel it is somehow familiar to them and will be more likely to buy it. This is called 'priming'. Your brain is primed to recognise something consciously because it has seen it before (even if you haven't consciously noticed it). Your brain notices much more, and much more quickly, than you can notice consciously.

When you have noticed something, you will recognize it more quickly when you see it again. Try folding a piece of paper in half, then in half again, again and again. Open out the paper and repeat the process as quickly as you can. It is so much quicker and easier the second time (you can even do it behind your back) because the paper is already creased in the right places. Similarly once your brain has formed neural links between pieces of information, it is easier for it to follow the same pathway the next time. You can do regular everyday tasks almost without thinking of them consciously at all.

We take advantage of this phenomenon when we're speed reading. When we preview a text, even just by flicking through it a couple of times, we are becoming familiar with it and it will be much easier to find information when we are consciously looking for it. Then while we're looking consciously for specific information, we are confident that our brain is also noticing other things. These may spontaneously come to mind later when we need them, or we may get a feeling that there's something else we need to check.

It is also why it is quicker and more effective to take a three-step approach to speed reading:
- preview a text
- work with the text to look for specific information
- rapid read through the whole text looking at every page (>p. 00)

Once your brain is primed with the first two steps, you can very quickly read through the whole text, being confident that you will notice things you may not have (consciously) noticed before.

Your conscious mind is the part of your brain you think you are thinking with right now – everything you are consciously aware of around you. However, at the same time as you are thinking about something with your conscious mind, other parts of your brain are taking note of everything else

Zigzag

- Put your finger at the top left of the page and then zigzag your way down the page.

- Depending on the density or complexity of the text, your zigzags can be wide and travel over several lines at a time, or more narrow, travelling over only 2 or 3 lines.

Your conscious mind is the part of your brain you think you are thinking with right now – everything you are consciously aware of around you. However, at the same time as you are thinking about something with your conscious mind, other parts of your brain are taking note of everything else around you. So while you're watching a film, advertisers are happy to pay large sums of money for their product to appear in the background, knowing that many people will notice it (even if not consciously) and therefore feel it is somehow familiar to them and will be more likely to buy it. This is called 'priming'. Your brain is primed to recognise something consciously because it has seen it before (even if you haven't consciously noticed it). Your brain notices much more, and much more quickly, than you can notice consciously.

When you have noticed something, you will recognize it more quickly when you see it again. Try folding a piece of paper in half, then in half again, again and again. Open out the paper and repeat the process as quickly as you can. It is so much quicker and easier the second time (you can even do it behind your back) because the paper is already creased in the right places. Similarly once your brain has formed neural links between pieces of information, it is easier for it to follow the same pathway the next time. You can do regular everyday tasks almost without thinking of them consciously at all.

We take advantage of this phenomenon when we're speed reading. When we preview a text, even just by flicking through it a couple of times, we are becoming familiar with it and it will be much easier to find information when we are consciously looking for it. Then while we're looking consciously for specific information, we are confident that our brain is also noticing other things. These may spontaneously come to mind later when we need them, or we may get a feeling that there's something else we need to check.

It is also why it is quicker and more effective to take a three-step approach to speed reading:
- preview a text
- work with the text to look for specific information
- rapid read through the whole text looking at every page (>p. 00)

Once your brain is primed with the first two steps, you can very quickly read through the whole text, being confident that you will notice things you may not have (consciously) noticed before.

Your conscious mind is the part of your brain you think you are thinking with right now – everything you are consciously aware of around you. However, at the same time as you are thinking about something with your conscious mind, other parts of your brain are taking note of everything else around you. So while you're watching a film, advertisers are happy to pay large sums of money for their product to appear in the background, knowing that many people will notice it (even if not con-

TO DO

Use the article "What Is Reading for?" (p.141) to practise these patterns.

1. Use super-reading to see how quickly you can find the following words (they appear sequentially):
   - human experience
   - social cohesion
   - relaxation
   - intertwined

2. Use the zigzag pattern with the article to see how quickly you can find the following words (they could be anywhere in the text - they are not necessarily in this order).
   - stress
   - complexities
   - journalism
   - misinformation

3. Randomly choose words from the index (p.172) and use any of the patterns to find the words as quickly as possible on the relevant page(s).

MORE ... if you need it

One more pattern: firsts and lasts

We mentioned before that you can look for summaries or hotspots of information (p. 14) in the first and last sections of a document.

You can also read the top line of each page and glance down the rest to see if anything relevant (a hotspot) jumps out at you – and then, if you need more information, read the beginnings and endings of sections or individual paragraphs. This will certainly help you find hotspots, and may also give you enough information to know you've understood the message of the text.

Author patterns

When previewing or reading a text, check what sort of pattern the author uses. It will help you find key information more quickly.

- Most writers tend to use the **first and last pattern** i.e. start with key message ... additional examples in the middle ... summary at the end.
- However, there are writers who start with a preamble, then they give the main message in the **middle of paragraphs**, and finish off with less important closing remarks (**middles**).
- Others build a case sequentially up to a conclusion (**lasts**).

How people look for information

You are probably already using some variation of these patterns when you read (or search through) information. Most people do - it's natural. The image below shows the places (the blobs) where people have gazed as they naturally look for hotspots of information in a text - identified by eye-tracking devices.

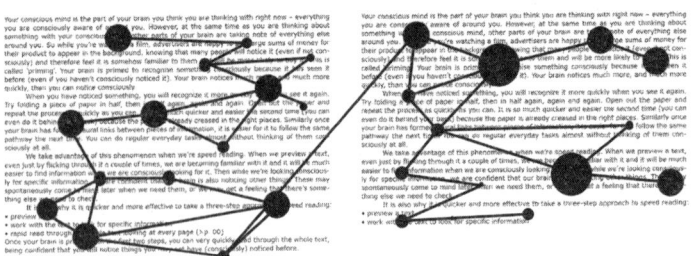

Your own patterns

While you're learning to speed read, use the patterns we've given you in this section to read sequentially, but as soon as you're comfortable with this way of finding information, feel free to experiment with any other pattern, such as a big question mark, seeing the page as a whole or glancing randomly down the page. You can also combine patterns. See what works for you - or what works better for different sorts of text.

From underlining to super-reading

While you're learning, it can be helpful to start with the underlining pattern because it's probably the pattern you're most used to. One way to build up to super-reading is to cut off the beginnings and endings of lines as you underline, and then gradually (over time, or over the course of a text you are working on) cut off more and more from the ends of each line until you are super-reading (moving your finger down the middle of the page with just a slight zigzag).

Remember, these patterns work because ...

- You are using the patterns to find hotspots of information (p.44), where you can zoom in and read for more detail.
- You are reading with a clear purpose (p.16), so you know what you're looking for.

- Your brain can get the general meaning of a text without seeing all the words in the right order.
- You don't have to focus on every word. Your brain can interpret words and phrases which you've seen in your peripheral vision (p.34).

Speeding up using different patterns

- You can use any of the 3 main patterns (underlining, super-reading, zigzagging) to get your eyes and brain up to speed before you start reading (p.71).
- If you are underlining (cutting off the beginning and ending of the line), then speed up at the rate of 1 second per line for a few pages - until you see some words and phrases as you flash past.
- If you are super-reading or zigzagging, speed up at the rate of 4 seconds per page for several pages.

Forward and backward

When underlining, if you go forward on one line and backward on the next, you're doing very tight zigzags. Try it first with texts in columns or short lines - by moving quickly you'll save time (not going back to the beginning each time) and understand groups of words even as you go backward.

Headings, bold text, pull quotes

Whatever pattern you're using, remember that you can always deviate slightly from the pattern to look at emphasized words such as headings or bold text.

TIP

Use a pacer! While you're underlining with your finger or moving your finger down the middle of the page for super-reading, your finger is acting as a "pacer". It sets the pace for your reading and reminds you to keep reading fast, while keeping track of where you've got to in the line or on the page. Instead of your finger, you can use a capped pen or anything else suitable.

You can also use your pacer down the side of a page, so it's not blocking the text.

You can use a pacer (your thumb, or a blank piece of paper or card) above the line you're reading, to block what you've already read, to discourage you from looking back and encourage you to look forward. Use a pacer any time you need one (e.g. with dense text or long lines, so you don't lose your place). If you don't need it, then stop.

QUIZ One

There are 6 basic principles underlying our approach to speed reading. These are the reasons we believe the speed reading techniques work. (We incorporate these principles into many other areas of our lives too.)

Use any of the speed reading techniques you know to answer the numbered questions as quickly as you can. (Clues on the opposite page.) Time yourself. Start now.

For the 6 questions below, find
a) the name of the principle
b) the page number on which you found it
c) the answer to the question (if required)

1. Which principle encourages you to stick to deadlines?
2. Which principle are advertisers particularly interested in?
3. When do you "zoom in"?
4. Which principle was popularized by Malcolm Gladwell?
5. Which principle discourages perfectionism?
6. Which idea would you use when looking for new learning?

Clues ... if you need them

- You can look up "Principles" in the Glossary/Index (p.172), or in the Contents.
- Read all the questions before you start looking through the principles.
- Skim quickly through each principle – as soon as you can match it to one of the questions, jot down the answer and move on to the next principle.
- One or more principles may appear after this quiz in the book.

  Check your answers on p.169.

TO DO (extra)

- Set your timer for 20 minutes.
- Look back at each principle and make sure you could explain it to someone else. (Take notes if necessary.)

Parkinson's Law

Parkinson's law is one of the key principles behind our approach to speed reading. It states that "*Work expands to fill the time available*". Conversely, if you limit the time available, you will work quicker (because you don't give yourself additional time "to be filled"). Working in 20-minute sessions encourages you to keep focused on the task, and in addition, most people work more quickly toward the end as they notice time running out.

The term "Parkinson's law" was first introduced by Cyril Northcote Parkinson in 1955. He illustrated it with the story of someone whose sole task for the day is sending a postcard – a task that only takes 3 minutes. Yet, by the time they've procrastinated, found the cards, chosen one, looked for their glasses, written the card, found a stamp and debated whether or not to take an umbrella to the postbox, this task has taken a whole working day.

In short, to combat Parkinson's law, employ strategies such as: planning your time, writing down your purpose, setting realistic deadlines, prioritizing tasks, breaking tasks into smaller steps and dedicating a specific time or amount of time to focus on completing each step.

The moral of the story: **set deadlines and timeframes, and stick to them**.

Take Notes ... with mindmaps and rhizomaps

SUMMARY We recommend taking notes as you read to help you remember what you read. Instead of writing down sentences, it is more effective to use keywords in mindmaps (when you know the structure of the information you are reading) or rhizomaps (when the structure is unknown).

INTRODUCTION Taking notes actively engages your mind, which helps you take in and understand information. It also helps you remember. We suggest that as you find useful information, you take notes using keywords. You can use any system of note-taking you like, but the mindmaps and rhizomaps we recommend here are flexible systems that will enhance your note-taking.

HOW TO ... mindmap and rhizomap

Use keywords

Whether you're taking audio notes or written notes, make sure you summarize the information in a few meaningful keywords (p.46) or key phrases. You are more likely to remember keywords because:

- your brain has been actively engaged in evaluating the information, understanding its meaning and choosing how to cut it down
- there's less to remember
- it takes longer to produce full sentences and play them back.

Exceptions

- You don't fully understand the sentence and you think it's important - then record the whole. thing, but go back as soon as possible to work out the meaning, and at that stage cut it down into keywords.
- You need the precise wording of certain ideas (e.g. definitions).
- It's a quote you want to use in its entirety. In this case, mark where the quote is, and go back when you've finished reading to copy it into the document where you want to use it.

Mindmapping

A mindmap starts with a central image or keyword representing the topic. Main "branches" radiate from this point, each with a word or phrase that sums up a core idea related to the topic. Further ideas and examples branch out as smaller "twigs". To help you remember, incorporate colours and pictures. A good mindmap expresses ideas concisely and uses branches to show how these ideas are interconnected.

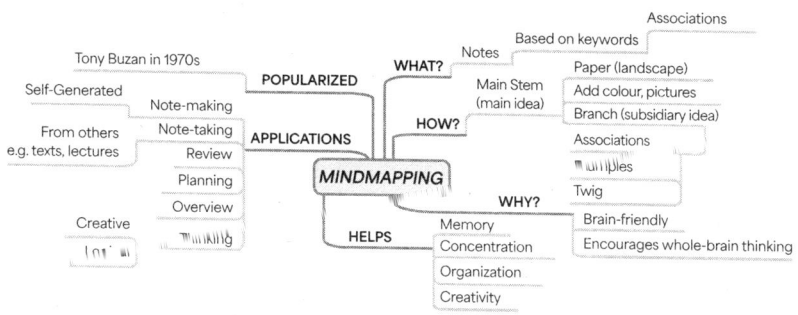

Rhizomapping

Rhizomapping is useful with a new subject when you don't know how the ideas are connected. As you find an idea, jot it down randomly. If another idea seems to be related, put it nearby. Alternatively, you can show connections during or after reading by adding arrows, colours or numbers.

After you have taken notes in a rhizomap, it can be helpful to spend a few minutes reorganizing it into a sequential mindmap. Reorganizing the information will help you remember it, and a mindmap is a clearer way of saving information in order to use it later, to explain the information to someone, write a report or prepare a presentation for example.

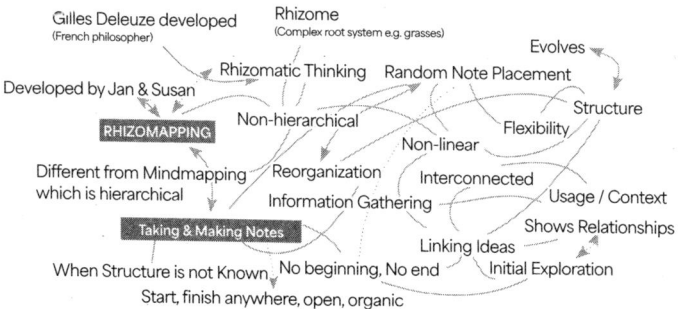

TO DO

Present this book as a mindmap – then compare it with ours (p.171).

Alternatively (or in addition) write your "to do" list as a rhizomap.

MORE ... if you need it

You can use both mindmaps and rhizomaps to:

- **take** notes – from another source, such as books, reports, lectures, etc. (keep the notes together with the text as a summary for later reference)
- **make** notes without an outside source, e.g. project planning, "to do" lists

Although there has been some research to indicate that people remember hand-written notes better than digital ones, there are mindmapping apps and programs available which are useful for storing information.

It can also be useful to make notes before you start reading (or listening to lectures, attending meetings, etc.). Jot down any questions you have or ideas you already think might be useful. This helps prepare your brain to understand the relevance of information you see or hear. You can do this by doing an outline mindmap, or with a "thought shower" (p.117), which is similar to a rhizomap.

"Train reading"

When you're away from your desk, on public transport or in waiting rooms, you can take temporary notes by:

- marking pages with Post-it notes – or bookmarking digitally
- highlighting relevant parts
- underlining manually – or digitally to add to crowd-sourced highlights (which are a good source of ready-made notes other people consider important)
- writing in the margins
- recording voice memos
- taking photos

Telling someone

After taking notes, explaining the information to someone else can help consolidate your thinking and help you remember. Saying the information out loud, as if to someone else, can also be useful.

Mindmaps were popularized by Tony Buzan in the 1970s. Feel free to adapt the system to suit yourself. Mindmaps are excellent when you already know what is important in a text and when information is presented (and captured) in a clear order. Traditionally a mindmap starts at the top right and follows round in a clockwise direction. See also: Building a "mindmap wall" (p.118).

80/20 Rule

The 80/20 rule, also known as the **Pareto principle**, is one of the key principles underlying speed reading. It states that **20% of effort gives 80% of results, while to achieve the remaining 20% of results takes 80% of effort.**

When it comes to speed reading, this means:

- With most texts, 80% of the message is contained in 20% of the words.
- Accept achieving 80% of your purpose, and use the time you save doing something else.
- You can speed read 5 books to 80% in the time it takes to read one completely.
- With most texts, you can ignore about 20% of the words because you don't need the information they contain.

The 80/20% discourages perfectionism. Perfectionism (wanting 100%) is an attitude which slows down the ability of many people to get **maximum information in the least possible time**. You don't need everything; you need "enough".

There are very few texts where the final 20% of information is worth more than the information you can get from reading 4 more texts. However, speed reading can still help you if you do need to read every single word (see Rapid reading p98, Legal documents p.124 and Proofreading p.116).

The Pareto principle was named by management thinker Joseph M Juran after the Italian economist Vilfredo Pareto, who observed in his garden that 80% of his peas were produced by 20% of peapods – and the remaining 80% of the peapods had many fewer peas. Pareto then realized that approximately 80% of his country's wealth went to 20% of the population. The principle applies in many other areas of life too:

- In business about 80% of sales come from 20% of customers.
- 80% of crime is committed by approximately 20% of criminals.
- 80% is around the grade needed to achieve a first class honours degree in most subjects at university.

 TECHNIQUE

20-Minute Sessions – putting it all together

This technique combines lots of the other techniques in a timed 20-minute session. It shows how things work together and why it's helpful to stick to time while you're learning speed reading.

Before the 20-minute session

You will have spent about 5 minutes:

- **previewing** your text and deciding that you want to work with it (p.10)
- setting your **purpose**, e.g. *to find 6 new ways of saving time when I'm working* (p.16)
- gathering everything you need to **take notes** (p.83) – preferably you'll have prepared a mindmap (or rhizomap) and written your purpose in the centre of it
- getting into a good **state** (p.61) including:
  - **opening your peripheral vision** (p.34)
  - **speeding up your eyes and your brain** (p.68)

HOW TO ... work in a 20-minute session

1. Set your timer for 20 minutes.
2. During the 20 minutes look through your text for 6 key points of information to **fulfil your purpose.** You can use the **contents list or index** to find sections, or flick through the text at random. Use **patterns** (p.71) to look through pages to **find hotspots** of information (p.44), if necessary **zooming in on** the text to read a bit more slowly to clarify meaning. When you find a point you want to remember, record it in your **notes** (p.83) and immediately move on to look for the next hotspot. Check the time occasionally to help you keep up momentum.
3. When the timer pings, stop.

Afterwards

4. Evaluate:
   - how much information you've got; if it's 80% of your purpose then congratulate yourself (p.88)
   - whether you will need this text for anything else – make a note if you do
   - how well you did the task – is there anything you would do differently and better next time?
   - whether you need more information (see over). If possible, to help you clarify and remember the information, **talk to someone** about it or speak the information out loud as if you were telling an appreciative audience.

TO DO

Find a text you genuinely need information from, with a real purpose. Have a 20-minute session to experience how much information you can get in the time.

If you are 80% successful, congratulate yourself, but even if not, the 20 minutes won't be wasted time because you'll have started finding your way around the text. Either way, work out what to do better next time and have another go soon.

MORE ... if you need it

Why 20 minutes?

- It's the optimum amount of time for adults to concentrate.
- You can get a lot of information in 20 minutes.
- Your optimal state lasts for approximately 20 mins (if not interrupted).
- Most people can find 20 minutes to dedicate to a task.

Stick to time

If you don't stick to time and your session runs on for another 10 minutes, you're less likely to stick to time for another session, and pretty soon you won't start a session (because you haven't got however many minutes you took last time) – and then you're back to slow reading. (See Parkinson's law p.82)

If you think you need more information

Sometimes you really do need to complete your stated purpose, in which case estimate how much more time you need to get the remaining information:

- If it's less than 5 minutes, take a 2- to 3-minute break and do it straight away.
- If it's more than 5 minutes, set up another work session after a break. Amend your purpose if necessary, and/or have a session which is less than 20 minutes long.

IF YOU THINK YOU'VE MISSED SOMETHING

Rapid read the text (p.98) and take note of what you missed. But if during this process, or with experience, you realize that what you've got is enough, then STOP. Be realistic; if you've got enough, it's enough. Spend the time you've saved to speed read something else.

Sometimes it's just a feeling that you've missed something. In the early days of speed reading, it's common to feel that you might have missed something important. Often it's **just a feeling** (because it doesn't feel like the reading you're used to), in which case:

1. Don't judge the process by your first experience – new skills can take some time to become second nature. Keep going.

2. Remember you're only aiming to achieve your purpose, not to get all the information from a text. You can always have another session with a different purpose.

3. Trust in the 80/20 rule (p.88) and accept what you've got if you think it's fulfilled your purpose to 80%.

4. Tell someone about what you've read. See how knowledgeable they think you sound.

5. Ask yourself, *"Do I really need every detail from this text?"* or *"Would it be more useful to get extra information elsewhere?"*, *"What exactly do I think I still need?"*, *"What's the worst that will happen if I have missed something?"*, *"Am I missing more by not reading other texts?"*

6. Read through the whole text in your pre-speed reading way, and see what you missed (it probably isn't worth doing that). Then, as soon as possible ...

7. Move on to another 20-minute session with another text and another purpose. As you get used to finding information quickly, the feeling will go away.

Also

- If a text has a lot of information, you can do more than one 20-minute session with it – but be careful you're not just breaking your text into 20-minute reads at your old speed. As long as you've looked through the whole text (during your preview p.10, or with your 20-minute session), then with your next purpose you will already know your way around the text which will help you find information more quickly.

- Stick to your stated purpose in this 20-minute session, and if you notice information that's useful for another purpose, mark it to come back to later.

- Mark it, then later copy/paste anything you want to quote directly into your work.

- If you find that you've got the wrong purpose (e.g. because the information you want turns out not to be there), change your purpose or change your text.

TIP

Always celebrate your successes! It's easy to focus on the negative (which is good if it helps you do something better next time, to learn and improve), but enjoying your success builds your motivation and confidence to do more.

Sameness And Difference

"Sameness" here means things you already know. "Difference" means something new. Sameness – repetition of things we know – can lead to greater understanding, or a deeper appreciation, particularly with difficult concepts, technical terms, philosophical ideas, etc.

When we read a new text, it is very tempting to look for or notice things that we already know (sameness) because they feel comfortable and make us feel validated.

However, when you are looking for new ideas in a text, look for difference – things that you don't already know. Learning new things, or gaining unique insights, is based on difference. In this case, you can overlook things you already know or things that are repeated (sameness). Experts, already knowledgeable in their field, seek new information as it is the new insights that will advance their extensive knowledge base.

For example, imagine moving through a city: each well-known landmark is like the "sameness" in your knowledge, while every new street or park gives you new, "different" insights. As a skilled speed reader, imagine yourself strategically plotting a route through a text, blending known information with new discoveries, building your understanding, like a city explorer expanding their map.

Add the word "new" to your reading purpose, e.g. "Discover 6 **new** techniques in online marketing" to focus your attention on finding innovative and distinct information within the field, and ensure that you specifically seek out fresh insights and ideas.

Recognizing sameness and difference is very beneficial when analyzing 2 or more texts on similar topics or the same subject.

Note: People share many characteristics, but they are also different in many respects (e.g. in their learning preferences, interests, experience, age, culture, etc.) so our approach to speed reading offers a variety of techniques and strategies, which build into a flexible system that can be adapted to different people and different types of text.

TECHNIQUE

Rapid Reading
... from cover to cover

SUMMARY Rapid reading means looking quickly at every page of a text from cover to cover. You usually do it after you have previewed the text and had a 20-minute work session. The purpose is both to get a consolidated overview of the message and to pick up any important details you might have missed. Depending on the length of the text, it usually takes about 20–45 minutes.

INTRODUCTION Rapid reading is possibly the simplest technique to do and it's what most people think speed reading is (if they haven't actually tried it). As we hope you've noticed from this book, with speed reading it's just as valid to go backward or forward through a text or only to specific sections for relevant information as it is to move through it sequentially.

One benefit (and use) of rapid reading is that it gives you an understanding of the sequence of events and how they lead one to another.

We've put rapid reading as one of the last techniques because it's much more effective when you know (and have used) the other techniques.

HOW TO ... rapid read

1. Turn the pages as quickly as you can from cover to cover, running your eyes down each page for about 2–10 seconds, noticing any important information. If there's something you need, mark it and keep rapid reading to the end.

2. If you marked any points as you were rapid reading, decide how long it will take you to get that information and either do it immediately (i.e. quickly take a note) or set it as your purpose for a separate work session.

TO DO

It's best to do this after you've tried out the other techniques in the book.

Rapid read this book, *Speed Reading Faster*. Notice techniques you know and can use – and anything else you hadn't properly noticed or thought about before. As you go, mark anything you want to take note of when you've finished rapid reading.

MORE ... if you need it

When to use rapid reading

- You might rapid read after you've done other techniques (e.g. previewing, and working with the book for at least one 20-minute session), and only if you feel you need to check that you haven't missed anything. Because you've worked with the book already, you will recognize most of the pages, and know what they're about and whether you need to read anything more. You can either consciously look for hotspots of key information or just notice anything you might have missed.

- Rapid reading can be the best technique for texts with a **continuous storyline** where you don't want to flick backward and forward, e.g. action stories (where you just want to know what happens), biographies and historical accounts (p.122).

  In this case, look sequentially through the book, using patterns (p.71) to skim through pages for information, then either zoom in (stop and read more slowly) when you reach hotspots, or mark the sections containing important information and go back to them in a later session.

- If you have a text where you have to follow a specific order to understand and reach a conclusion, we recommend reading the first and last sections (so you know the start and finish points), then rapid read the whole text. Slow down and zoom in if there are difficult sections that you don't understand straight away – or mark them to go back to once you've got the full overview.

- New speed readers often do rapid reading to reassure themselves that they haven't missed anything. As you grow to trust the process (and your own brain), you are likely to use it less and less for this purpose.

- Experienced speed readers might do rapid reading after previewing and setting a purpose, but before (or instead of) a 20-minute work session with a text. In this case, we often rapid read before we go to sleep, knowing that our peripheral vision will take in more information than we can see consciously, and our brains will be primed to process some of that information while we sleep. Then in the morning we can find answers and information in the document more quickly.

- **Train reading:** We often rapid read when we're travelling and it's impractical to have a work session. We usually rapid read texts that we're interested in reading, but where we haven't got a clear purpose or need, e.g. background reading around a subject. Depending on the length of the journey, and how easy it is to access the information, we might spend a bit longer on each page. We still mark words, ideas or sections to go back to later.

- **Last-minute panic:** Rapid reading can be the choice technique when there's something big you need to read urgently before an important event, such as an interview, meeting or exam (i.e. something you should really have started some time ago). In this case, set a goal rather than a purpose (p.21), e.g. *to pass the exam tomorrow, to have answers to impress the boss/ interviewer/client/jury*. Before you start rapid reading, take a breath, relax and smile (it's a good idea to have practised getting into a good state in advance too!), and then trust that the information you need will enter your brain and be available to you at the right time. Get into a good state again just before the event.

Note: These last-minute suggestions can work for anyone, especially if they are relaxed and focused (i.e. not stressed), but they work best if you have some experience with lots of the other speed reading techniques. However, don't expect to remember this information once the important event is over.

TIP

Speed readers turn pages more quickly. As soon as you've turned a page and while you're reading, get the next page ready for a quick turn. (It saves more time than you'd think!)

Syntopic Processing – 4 texts in 75 minutes

SUMMARY "Syntopic" means a combination (synthesis) of topics, and syntopic processing means working with several texts on the same or similar subjects, all with the same purpose. It only takes 75 minutes, and is a way of comparing, contrasting and analyzing multiple texts simultaneously to synthesize knowledge from various perspectives. Use any relevant speed reading techniques to work with each of the texts.

INTRODUCTION There is usually quite a lot of overlap in the content of texts on the same or similar subjects. This means that it can save a lot of time to speed read several texts in one work session.

HOW TO ... work with 4 texts

1. **Define your purpose** (p.16). Have one central purpose for the 4 texts. Aim for a total of 11 pieces of key information from the texts.
2. **Select and preview texts.** Choose 4 relevant texts. Quickly preview each (2-3 minutes per book) to ensure they contain information to fulfil your purpose.

103

3. **Prepare the outline of a mindmap or rhizomap** (p.83). Write your purpose in the middle. You can organize your notes around the texts/books (see example below) or just write the ideas you want to extract from the material.

4. **Get into a good state** (p.61).

5. **Set your timer and work with the first text for 15 minutes** - gather as many points as possible to fulfil your purpose. At the end of 15 minutes STOP (even if you think there's more to get).

6. **Work with your second text for 15 minutes.** If you find that this text (or any of the texts) is not giving you the information you want, stop working with it and move to the next text.

7. **Take a short stretch break.**

8. **Work with the final 2 texts for 15 minutes each.**

9. **In your final 7 minutes, evaluate** how much information you still need and, if necessary, look back at the text you think will give you that information.

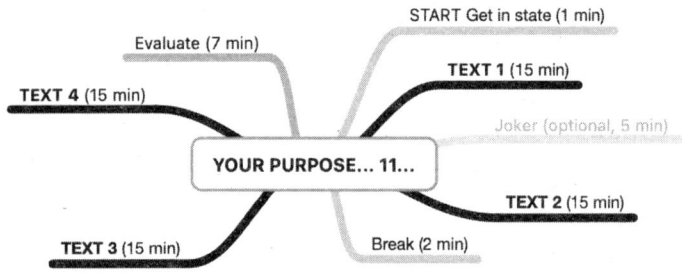

TO DO

If you're currently working on a project, gather your texts and have a 75-minute session.

If not, choose a topic you're curious about and select 4 texts to explore - it can be fun to see how much information you can get in such a short time.

MORE ... if you need it

- **Similarities and contrasts.** Pay attention to recurring themes (these are things that are generally agreed on), contradictions and unique viewpoints from the different texts.

- **Notes** can either be organized according to the book you took them from (with each book in its own space or branch), or according to the important ideas (with each idea on a branch) - in which case you might want to use initials and page numbers to identify where you took the ideas from. If you note down page references, always write down what the page refers to, otherwise you'll have to spend a lot of time looking everything up again.

- **Artificial Intelligence (AI)** can do syntopic processing by swiftly analyzing and synthesizing key information from multiple digital texts. Upload the different texts into your AI tool and use prompts based on your purpose, such as "Analyze and synthesize these texts", or "Compare and contrast these texts based on [my research question]", or "Take information from these texts to give an overview of the subject". Evaluate the AI's answer and adjust your prompts if necessary.

EXTRA ... incorporating a "joker"

This is an optional but recommended addition to the syntopic process. To stimulate creative thinking, include a random, seemingly unrelated book in your session (like the joker in a pack of cards) and spend a few minutes considering how this "joker" might offer unique insights into your subject. It can foster your creativity and inspire new ways to approach the process of learning and the end result, and a fun jokey book can encourage a positive mental state which is good for learning. We keep a selection of joker texts for an element of surprise and novelty in our speed reading classes, including a children's recipe book, collections of quotations, essays, jokes, sayings and poems, mini-dictionaries, phrasebooks and small directories on history, wildflowers and birds. Some ideas our students have got from jokers are: "I can lighten up and enjoy this more", "I could structure my presentation like a recipe book", "Lists and bullet points would make my content more accessible". Several people have taken useful suggestions for their purpose, and one person completely changed his approach to the subject because of the joker. If you use a joker, put it in after the first book - treat it as a source of information for your purpose, and spend a maximum of 5 minutes on it.

Pleasure Reading

SUMMARY The easiest "purpose" (p.16) for reading is pleasure. If that is your purpose, choose something which gives you pleasure (based on recommendations, previous experience, or even "previewing" p.10) and read it in any way that gives you pleasure, in your leisure time (which is why it's sometimes called "leisure reading").

INTRODUCTION You may well get pleasure from speed reading more efficiently and effectively, and you can use speed reading techniques to get information from books you enjoy, e.g. for self-development or your hobbies. But in this section we are focusing on fiction and we are assuming that you're reading in your leisure time – which could include "train reading" (reading while travelling or waiting around).

Stories
If you just want to know what happens, you can skip the descriptive bits and focus on the action. If you want to snuggle up and immerse yourself in the story, read as much detail as you like, as quickly or slowly as you like.

So, go faster in the bits you find boring, and slow down in those bits you want to savour.

Poetry

Since poetry often captures the essence of an idea, and the way it is written may be an important part of its meaning, you may want to savour every word as you read slowly, possibly reading aloud to enjoy the sounds and rhythms of the language. As with religious or philosophical texts, poetry isn't easy to speed read and you may want to read it more than once.

For anyone just starting to read for pleasure

- Read a summary or simplified version of the story before watching or reading a play (e.g. Shakespeare).
- Audiobooks will give you the story – try listening and reading the text at the same time.
- Build your confidence by reading books that are considered simple or easy "for your age", like simplified versions of stories written for foreigners (with simplified vocabulary).
- Children's books can be delightful (especially if you're reading them to a child).
- Books for young adults can be enjoyable in their own right.
- Comics are fun, and the pictures give you half the story.
- Try making pictures in your head to imagine the scene and what the characters look like.

MORE ... if you need it

- Pleasure depends on your mood – so read at whatever pace feels comfortable and enjoyable.
- The first few pages (or even couple of chapters) of a book are the most difficult to read because everything is new – characters, setting, the style of writing. Keep reading past the second chapter to really give it (and yourself) a fair go. How often have you heard someone say "I loved it once I got into it"?
- Studying literature is different from reading literature for pleasure. Treat your studies as work sessions: use summaries to get an overview, compare your opinions with other people's, etc. You can read these texts for pleasure later when you have the time – hopefully the greater understanding you gained from your studies will bring you a deeper pleasure.
- At the end of the day, if it's not giving you pleasure, stop. You don't owe the author anything. Find something you'll enjoy reading more.
- See also "How to Remember" (p.128)

TIP

Don't try to get information from a text while you're reading for pleasure – pleasure always wins. You'll still have to read it again for information. But you can do both at different times.

Speed Reading For Study

This section is for anyone of any age following a course of study, including students going to college or university.

Your motto should be "Be prepared". Get ahead of the game and stay relaxed. But if it's too late for that, go straight to "last-minute panic" at the end of this section.

We start with basic notes, then give real-life examples of how our students have used speed reading techniques to study more efficiently (they saved a lot of time) and effectively (they learned their subject and passed exams). If necessary, go back to the pages where the techniques are described in detail.

Many of the suggestions are also relevant to older school students - if this is you, have a look at "Textbooks" (p.122), and if you are answering comprehension questions about a text, you can use these questions as your purpose (p.16).

HOW TO ... speed read for study

- Preview all your reading lists (p.14).
- Make overview mindmaps of each subject (p.83) and, as time goes on, a mindmap for each aspect of the subject (see p.118 - **"Building a mindmap wall"**, to cover a subject in detail).

- Prepare for lectures and tutorials with 20-minute work sessions with a relevant book – your purpose could be *6 ideas about the title of this lecture.* (If you go to a lecture without preparing you'll spend much longer sorting out your notes afterwards). If you don't have 20 minutes, spend a few minutes preparing your mind before the session with a **thought shower** (see p.117).
- Get into a good state (p.61), open your peripheral vision (p.34), and speed up your brain and your eyes (p.68) – do all of this regularly so it will be second nature when it comes to combating exam nerves.
- Rapid read (p.98) additional background texts or texts with sequential storylines – either in spare moments (e.g. on public transport – "train reading") or before sleep.
- Revise – using past papers and making mindmap notes for essays (see p.116).
- If you're out of time, go to the "Last-minute panic" section (p.120).
- To help you find your way into texts and subjects, and to get opinions and quotes from other people, use online introductions and summaries or published notes.

MORE ... if you need it

Student speed reading experiences

Below are some examples of what our students have said about their speed reading successes. All of them used all the speed reading techniques from this book.

Adam's experience

Adam was one of our most successful students. He took the speed reading course with us about 3 weeks before he started his university master's degree.

*"I had **previewed** all the books on the reading list before I got to uni so I knew which ones to go to for the different aspects of the subject. I went into my first seminar having done a **syntopic processing** (p.103) session with 4 books on the subject (the **purpose** (p.16) was the title of the seminar). None of the other students had read more than half a book – not necessarily the best book – and they knew almost nothing about the subject. I already knew at least 80% of what the tutor told us, which meant I was able to take part in a meaningful discussion. From that moment on, the other students were all playing catch-up while I had the time to keep ahead of the game – which was essential when the lecturers seemed to be expecting us to read up to 30 books a week! (How does anyone do that without speed reading?)*

*I prepared for (almost) every seminar, lecture and essay in the same way: **syntopic processing** – or a **20-minute session** (p.90) with a key book – often adding ideas from additional books which I thought the tutors might find challenging! If I was short of time before a lecture, I'd just do a quick **thought shower** (see p.117) and prepare an **outline mindmap** (p.83) with things I knew (sometimes while I was waiting for the lecture to start). But I was able to listen critically and just take occasional notes while everyone else was frantically writing down everything – often in full sentences – so they had to go through everything again afterwards. They didn't know which bits were important. I did.*

*I did extra background reading when I was travelling or waiting in queues (you called it **train reading**).*

*I'm pretty laid-back anyway, but I always got into a **good state** (deep breath, relax, open peripheral vision, smile, pause and plan) and did the **speeding up** technique (p.67) before any reading or learning task. By the time exams came round, it was second nature to me and I kept exam nerves to a minimum.*

That was a hectic year, but I managed to keep my sanity (and a full-time job) and get a good degree. I also feel I really got to know and understand my subject."

Jan's experience

Even though Jan is an excellent speed reader, when he was researching for his master's degree, he used the **search facility** on his laptop with nearly 100 papers, which he filed in one folder, to find information relevant to his subject. It would have taken him 10 times as long to find and then look through the same amount of material on his own. Today he would also be able to use AI tools to write up all his sources and references in the correct format.

It took Jan 4 false starts with books supposedly aimed at beginners (Jan ordered them online and wasn't able to **preview** properly) before he found one that explained the subject of statistics clearly. He started by making an overview **mindmap** (p.83) of the whole subject, sticking it up in the middle of a blank wall. (This actually took 27 minutes.) There were 6 main chapters and therefore 6 branches of the mindmap, each representing one aspect of statistics. He'd skimmed through each chapter to know roughly what it was about and to add a few notes to each branch of the mindmap.

He spent a **20-minute session** on each chapter, and produced an overview summary of each. He added these to the wall around the first mindmap.

Next he worked through the "study questions" at the end of each chapter. He did a 20-minute session (or less) for each question, with the purpose "6 key ideas to answer [title of question]". He scanned through the chapters of the book using different **patterns** (mainly **zigzag** and **super-reading**), **zoomed in** to read more slowly for useful information and added notes to the mindmap. He found the first question in each chapter quite hard, but the next questions covered things he'd already read for an earlier question, so they got easier and took less time to answer. The bonus was that he was learning the information in the same way he would have to present it in the exam.

Jan was used to getting into a good **state**, which meant he was calm in the exam before he turned the paper over – and he sipped water throughout the exam. With the multiple choice answers he didn't know, he guessed – often correctly.

Jan's goal was simply to pass the statistics exam. Once he'd found the right book, the whole process took him a day and a half, working in 20-minute sessions with breaks of 5-15 minutes, plus meal breaks. On the 2 evenings (one in the middle of study and one before the exam) he **rapid read** through the whole book (which took half an hour) before he went to sleep.

He would barely have been able to read the whole book sequentially in a day and a half using traditional reading – and he certainly wouldn't have had time to actually learn and remember much about the subject. In the end, while some people who had been studying statistics for 3 years failed, he got a good pass with 70%.

MORE suggestions for students

Essay writing

This book is about reading rather than writing; however, we'd like to offer a couple of tips:

1. As soon as you get your essay title, spend 5 or 10 minutes jotting down everything you can think of which might be included in your answer - probably as a **thought shower** or **rhizomap**. This will prime your brain to notice related information you might come across - and it will continue to do this until the task is finished. You might find useful ideas popping into your mind at odd times when you're doing something else - always make a note of them and add them to your rhizomap as soon as possible.

2. About a week before the essay is due, have a **syntopic processing** (p.103) session to collect ideas and quotations from 4 different texts.

3. When you start writing, start with the main body of the essay, putting the information from your rhizomap and syntopic processing session in a coherent order. The last thing to write is a clear introduction and ending.

4. Finally, **proofread** your essay twice - once from the beginning to make sure the ideas make sense and a second time to check things like grammar, spelling and punctuation. For the second read, you're more likely to pick up mistakes if you start in the middle, work through to the end and then go back to the

beginning and work through to where you started. (Most people read from the beginning and begin to miss things at the end when they're getting tired.) Also, double-check headings and any last-minute changes – they are often the source of errors.

HOW TO ... thought shower

If you don't have time to prepare properly, even a few minutes' preparation is worth doing. You can do a "thought shower" while you're sitting waiting for the lecturer to begin. Just jot down any ideas you think the lecture is going to be about and any questions you hope will be answered. Even if you're wrong, your brain will be primed and better prepared to understand and absorb information.

first idea

What do I know
about this?

another idea

What's it about?

idea

'thought shower'

....

(title of lecture here)

idea

my questions?

....

lots of ideas

....

HOW TO ... learn and revise
using past exam papers

As soon as possible on your course, study for the final exam using questions from past exam papers. If you're asked to read without a specific purpose, choose a question to answer about that topic as your purpose and look for answers to the question. This way you'll always be learning information in context.

When revising, also choose 4 or 5 past exam questions on each topic. For the first question, all your facts will be new. By the second and third questions, there will almost certainly be some overlap - certain facts will be useful for answering more than one question, and your task will be getting easier. With questions 4 and 5 there will be a lot of overlap and you'll have a good knowledge of the subject.

HOW TO ... build a mindmap wall

In order to get your head around a whole subject, start by making a mindmap overview - the main branches are often based on chapters in a textbook.

The subject of each main branch then becomes the starting point for another mindmap where you will probably add more detail. Any of the main branches of each of those mindmaps can then become the centre of additional mindmaps. You will not necessarily add to all the branches equally - you may decide to go into much greater detail in some areas, but at all times you can see how the details fit into the big picture.

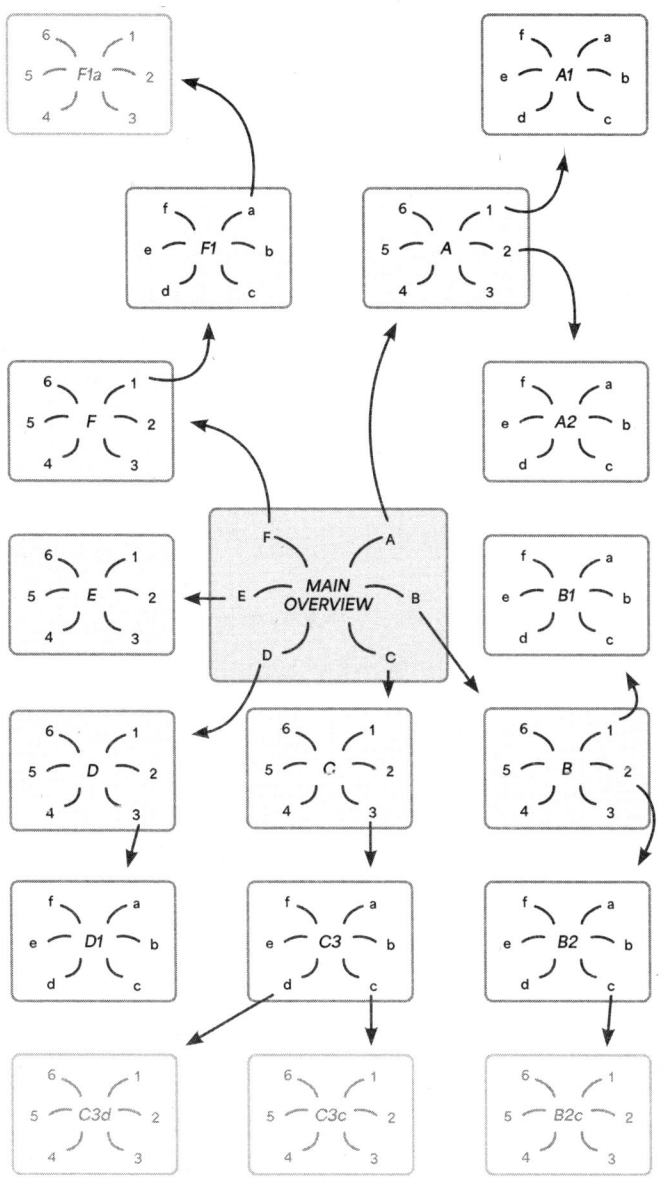

Recreate your original mindmap

If you have already created a mindmap, you can try and recreate it from memory to revise and test yourself. Start with a blank piece of paper and see how much you can recall as you reconstruct your original mindmap. Compare your reconstruction with your original and add in anything you've missed. When you repeat the exercise, you'll probably find that you forget different things.

The only way to build recall is to practise recall. Just reading through your notes is a relatively passive activity – your brain needs to be actively engaged to build memory. (See also "How to Remember" p.128.)

Last-minute panic

Speed reading techniques work best if you have practised with them in advance – so work through this book, preferably before you start your course.

However, if you have come to this book in a panic because you haven't got time to do anything, then turn to the "Last-minute panic" section (p.101) and read the summary, introduction and HOW TO sections for the rapid reading technique (p.98).

If you have a bit more time, go through the 3 main speed reading techniques in the book (preview p.10, purpose p.16, getting into a good state p.61) – read the summaries, introductions and HOW TO sections, and practise each technique with the TO DO suggestion, and/or put it into practice with texts on your subject.

Speed Reading Different Kinds Of Text

INTRODUCTION Do you read emails, digital text messages, self-help books, novels and computer manuals all in the same way? Hopefully not. All of them can be read conventionally (and slowly), but there are different ways of approaching all of them which will speed up the process. **Self-help books** are an ideal starting point for practising speed reading skills since they usually make it relatively easy to find strategies you can put into practice.

Everything in this section assumes that you are **reading for information** (see p.107 for reading for pleasure); that you will be using the basic speed reading techniques outlined in this book; that you have a clear **purpose** (p.16) for each text; that you will get into a good **state** (p.61), open your peripheral vision (p.34) and **speed up** (p.68) your eyes and your brain; also that you know, when needed, how to **preview** (p.10), use **patterns** (p.71) to look for **hotspots** of key information (p.44), **skim for meaning** (p.19) and **scan for specific information** (p.19), have **20-minute work sessions** (p.90), **take notes using mindmaps or rhizomaps** (p.83), and **rapid read** from cover to cover (p.98). Additional specific suggestions follow.

HOW TO approach ...

Digital reading

All the speed reading techniques can be used with digital texts as well as hard copies. Use the **search function** to find known keywords and concepts. Also remember you can change the font and size of the text to one you find easiest to read. (See also "AI" p.159)

Textbooks

If textbooks include questions at the end of sections, you can use these questions as your purpose for scanning through that section, looking specifically for information to answer each question.

If the text is written in note form, then the key information has already been extracted for you – the challenge now is how to remember it. For that, the trick is to bring the notes to life by imagining them in real-life situations which you can picture in your mind's eye. You can also rearrange the notes as mindmaps to show the connections, and add real-life examples and pictures to your mindmap. See other suggestions in "How to Remember" (p.128) and the section on study (p.110).

History, biographies and other sequential information

It can be harder to extract information when it is written within a sequential storyline – as is the case with history books and accounts of the development of people (biographies), companies, products or ideas.

Start by previewing to see how important the storyline is, where facts are located and how hard it is to identify them. Consider making notes (a mindmap, rhizomap or thought shower) of anything you already know or expect to find. A timeline can often be helpful too. If the text is written in chronological chapters, either skim through each chapter to find the message and jot down a quick summary, or have a work session with a clear purpose for each chapter. If following the entire storyline is important, then instead (or as well) you might rapid read the book (p.98) to get an overview of the story, and mark the sections you want to return to once you've got to the end – this may be a 2-step process: rapid read to get an overview of the storyline, take a break, then rapid read again, marking the sections you want to take information from. You can then have work sessions with a clear purpose, concentrating on the key information you need.

Emails (and other digital messaging)

Every time your concentration is interrupted, it can take up to 10 minutes to refocus on a task, so unless there is a particularly important email or text you are waiting for, look at them at regular intervals – e.g. every 20 minutes when you've finished another task – rather than as soon as they arrive. Our method is to skim through them and:

- respond immediately to urgent and important messages
- ignore non-work until you have some free time

- deal with anything which can be done in under 2 minutes
- allocate more time to emails that will take longer to respond to and slot them into your day depending on their urgency.

Case studies, legal documents and scientific papers

These all have typical layouts. Your first task is to preview them to establish that layout and discover where to find the introduction, contents lists, index, conclusions and summaries which you can then skim for meaning. If you need to know or evaluate how results or conclusions were reached, read the descriptive content. How much you need to read depends on (a) your experience with the subject and (b) what you need the information for. This book has largely covered how to get the information.

If you have little experience with the subject then read the section on study (p.110) for how to expand your learning and expertise quickly.

You may find it useful to work out your own way of summarizing and recording the document for yourself as an adapted mindmap or chart – having a regular place to note key facts that you would expect to find and a place for questions that you think may not have been answered.

When you understand what the text contains, ask yourself the question "What's missing?" Something that hasn't been explained, or which has been avoided, may be the key to something more important than what has been written.

Once you have done this, if you need to read every word (e.g. in a contract), then see rapid reading (p.98) and proofreading (p.116).

Very long manuals and documents

If the document is online, use AI to get a synopsis overview and then to search for specific information. It can also compare a previous version of the document with this one for updates. Check whether anyone else has already extracted key points or summarized sections which you could look at.

Preview a hard copy of the text to find out how easy it is to navigate, how useful the headings are, whether it has a contents list and index, and where you can find summaries, introductions, conclusions and recommendations (which you will read first).

If it can be divided into separate sections, look at each section separately and decide on a purpose for each section. If you are searching for specific information, you can use the index or headings to find the right area, using patterns to scan for hotspots.

Add your own notes, headings or summaries in case you need to use the document again.

Manuals (e.g. computer manuals)

Most manuals are available digitally these days, so it is relatively easy to find specific information, but with any practical subject, set yourself a practical task and then have a reading session to find out how to do that task, and if possible actually do the task. Once you've skimmed through the steps of what you have to do, it's perfectly sensible to have the text open and follow the instructions as you put them into practice, just as you would expect to have the recipe open while you make a cake for the first time. Build up your knowledge and experience with subsequent tasks.

Journals, magazines, newspapers

Since these are composed of numerous articles about different subjects, preview first (p.10) to identify which ones you want to skim through (to keep up to date) or consider in more detail, after which you can dispose of them or store them if you need them for reference.

Dictionaries, encyclopedias, etc.

Dictionaries, encyclopedias and other books containing varied pieces of unrelated information about different subjects are specifically written so you can easily look up information when you need it. They can also be fun to dip into at random from time to time just to find interesting facts. It isn't easy to read (or speed read) them like a sequential story - the topic keeps changing, and every entry is like a summary because it is packed with information, so you'll need to read those a bit more slowly, but you can still use speed reading skills to check what the books contain and to find specific information.

Philosophical, religious or spiritual texts

Although it is possible to use speed reading techniques to navigate these texts or find your way into them, the challenge is to reach a deeper understanding of the possible meanings of the content – people spend a lifetime studying such texts. Speed reading skills can also be useful for summarizing other people's writings with their interpretations of these texts, with the purpose of enhancing your own understanding or ideas.

Mathematical formulae

Although speed reading is useful for identifying and reading information about mathematical formulae, you will need to work with a formula in order to understand it fully, and probably also learn the simpler ones by heart.

We suggest you use this article, after you have been through all the techniques, as your "3-minute second read" to see how much more quickly and effectively you're reading (see Speed Test on p.146).

Afterwards, set your timer to 4 minutes and go quickly through the article, taking notes about things which are relevant to your reading. If you notice anything else useful, have a further 4-minute read to take notes.

How To Remember

Your brain is very good at forgetting. It regularly edits whatever you encounter in your day and chooses to forget certain details, especially things you do regularly. (Do you remember the details of cleaning your teeth every day?) Shedding information, or letting information drop down in terms of importance, means that the brain has more "pathways" free to do other tasks. We therefore tend to remember things which are out of the ordinary or special in some way, particularly if a strong emotion is attached or your senses are involved. The brain also remembers things which are important to your survival. (You don't need to put your hand in a fire more than once to remember not to do it again.) [121 words]

In general, although you might think your job or an exam are important, your brain might not agree, and therefore will not necessarily retain any information you read unless you make an active effort to remember it. With reading, understanding is an important first step, but it's not enough to build a memory. [53 words/174 total]

In order to remember you need first to choose or notice what it is that you want to remember. Then actively do something so that your brain forms enough connections between the new piece of information and existing information for the memory to be easily retained. Finally you need to make sure you have a "trigger" to be able to find that experience, word or piece of information quickly and easily. Also you need to be mentally alert – memories are not easily formed when you are ill, tired or under the influence of drugs or alcohol. Being in a good state (p.61) makes it easier to concentrate, and therefore to understand and remember anything, including what you read. [118 words/total 292]

Remembering what you read

The first steps in forming a memory of what you read are setting a purpose and taking notes.

Setting a purpose before you start reading helps you clarify what you think is important and you are therefore more likely to take notice of the information you want to remember. Asking yourself questions as you read (and before and after reading) also helps keep your brain active and focused. [72 words/total 364]

Taking notes means that your brain has interacted with the information, through choosing what is important, and by interacting with the ideas as it reduces sentences or ideas to keywords. When the notes are in the form of a mindmap, the brain is also choosing how the ideas are interconnected. With traditional sequential notes where the original sentences are often written out in full, it has been said that "the ideas move from the notes of the lecturer to the notes of the student without passing through the mind of either". If you don't think about your notes as you write them, you're going to need to think much harder about their meaning later. You need to engage with notes as you take them. [124 words/total 488]

On the other hand, trying to remember everything you read as you read will slow down your reading significantly. It's better to understand the information as quickly as you can and take notes. Then decide whether you need to take further steps to remember. [44 words/total 532]

Remembering what you read for pleasure

There are various methods to remember what you're reading for pleasure. If the names and relationships are complicated, make quick notes of them as you go, until you're confidently embroiled in the story (by which time you probably won't need them). As you go along, you can bring the story to life – and make it more memorable – by imagining (making pictures in your head – like a film) the characters, their surroundings and the things that happen to them. Alternatively, wait till the end of a page/section/chapter and quickly summarize what's happened – in words (possibly taking physical notes) and/or mental pictures. [109 words/total 641]

If you are having trouble following the sequence of a story, stop to make a mental picture of whatever's happening, and then create a strong visual link between that scene and the one you move on to next. This is particularly helpful when you're reading historical stories, both fiction and fact. If you're reading a biography, picture the person looking older as you go through their life. [67 words/total 708]

When you finish the book, write a short "review" and keep it with any notes you made earlier. [18 words/total 726]

Review and revision

Review and revision essentially mean the same thing: look again. Looking at things again is a good way of sending a message to your brain that this is something you want to be able to remember. And when we say we want to remember something, we usually mean that we want to be able to recall it at will. [62 words/total 788]

There are two ways you can purposefully trigger a memory in your brain. One is to look at it again, and your brain essentially says "Yep, I remember that". This is why it's relatively easy to recognize people and know that you've seen them before. However, it's not necessarily so easy to remember their names. That's because you have to bring the information to mind without looking at the face you recognize. This is the other way to trigger a memory: recall. And the only way to build the ability to recall is to practise recall. Reading through notes again and again is a very tiresome and relatively useless way of revising. It is much more effective to practise recalling the information, e.g. by reconstructing your mindmap from memory, and then checking to see what you forgot. If you do this more than once, you usually find that each time you remember the things you forgot last time – because you've put extra emphasis on them – and forget other things. Usually after three reviews you find that you know the information. [180 words/total 968]

There are optimal periods of time for you to review information – basically after 1 day, 1 week and 1 month. People who make no particular effort to remember information forget, on average, about 90% within 48 hours. (Therefore 2 people who have read the same book, or been to the same lecture, could effectively remember completely different things.) However, if you review (practise recall) after 1 day, you can bring your memory back to almost 100% of what you want to remember. Similarly after a week and a month. If you look at the diagram, you'll see that each time you bring your memory back to 100% it takes a bit longer to forget, and in the meantime much more of the information has been available to you, and your brain will have been making links between this and other things you have been thinking about. The more neural links your brain makes, the stronger the memory, and also the easier it is to retrieve – recall – the information. [168 words/total 1136]

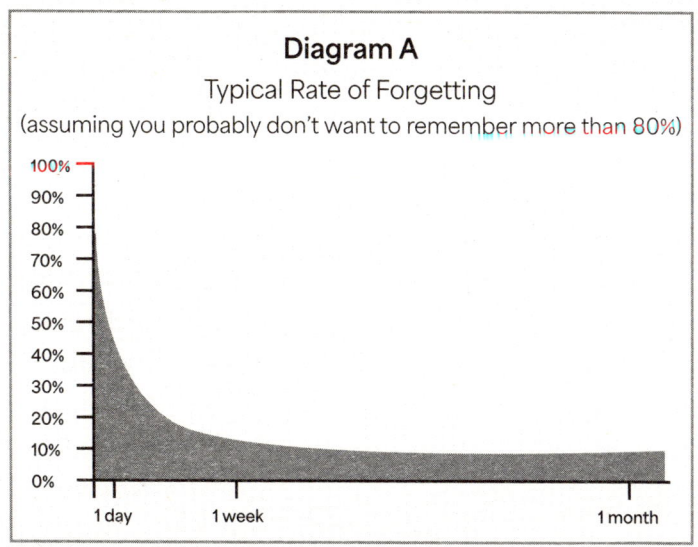

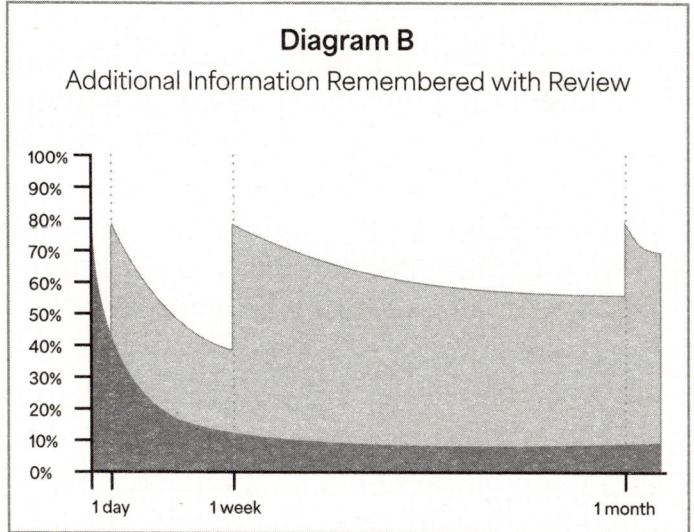

[25 words/total 1161]

Personal memories

With personal memories we might keep a diary, a journal or a blog to remember things that happened and how we felt about them, or take photos, keep mementos and make scrapbooks. This is the active part of creating the memories. Creating these things involves making a choice about what we want to remember. Looking back at these things triggers the associated memories. Anything you do or use to help you remember is known as an "aide-mémoire" (French for "memory aid"). [83 words/total 1244]

People also spontaneously experience strong memories triggered by any of their senses – cooking smells in a hot street might transport you back to a foreign holiday, a particular flower might bring a strong memory of your grandmother, and famously the author Marcel Proust recorded that eating a small cake called a madeleine unlocked his protagonist's memories in his work *In Search of Lost Time* (*À la recherche du temps perdu*). [70 words/total 1314]

Remembering names and faces

It is usually much easier to remember faces than names. This is because our brain is much better at recognizing pictures (faces, places, objects) than it is at recalling names (words and information). Recognition is easier than recall. [42 words/total 1356]

If you want to remember names, the trick is to find a visual reference, such as something or someone else they remind you of – someone you know personally, or because they're famous. Then look carefully at their features and picture this person with the person you know. Break their surname into parts and see if the whole name or one of its parts is something you can imagine (i.e. form an image of in your mind). George Greenfield is a relatively easy example – actor George Clooney, or if you have a friend called George, for the first name, then imagine him standing in a wide field of green grass (green grass for the initials GG). Another example, Sandra Armstrong – imagine Sandra Bullock (actress) showing off her arm muscles. Make sure you're imagining the person's face alongside the image you have created for their name (remember the face because people change their hair and clothes). Surname Cheyney – imagine the person with a chain around one knee. Surname L'Estrange – sounds French, Le Stranger (imagine the person being strange). Collier – imagine a collie dog around their neck like a collar. It's trickier with less obvious names, or names not from your culture, but find something you can link with the name and exaggerate it as you form a mental picture linked to their face. [221 words/ total 1577]

Make sure you say the person's name more than once in your first encounter, and if possible discuss the name and its spelling and pronunciation. The reason we often don't remember names is that we don't really pay attention in the first place. [43 words/total 1620]

Imagining and linking

Imagining is more memorable if you make your mental picture out of the ordinary in some way, e.g. exaggeration (make the thing huge), highly coloured, a cartoon version, etc. The sillier or funnier the better (i.e. the more memorable) it will be. If you can bring in other senses, so much the better – add sound, movement, smells, how something feels or tastes. It is easier to remember – and especially to recall – something if you create links with things you already know. The more links you have the better. [91 words/total 1711]

Foreign vocabulary

You can use the name linking system for words in a foreign language. For example, to learn the German word for "duck" (*Ente*), you imagine a large comedy duck "enter-ing" through a door. To learn the Spanish for "waitress" (*camarera*), imagine a waitress with an old-fashioned camera hanging round her neck. The French for "fish" is *poisson* – imagine somebody poisoning a goldfish in a bowl. [67 words/total 1778]

Remembering your keys

It's easier to remember where you left your keys/glasses/bag/ or TV remote if you always put them back in the same place (on the hall table, in your right-hand pocket, etc.), and as you put them down notice, or take a mental picture of, the things around the item (we often focus on the thing itself, which won't help us find it). When you park your car, look around for landmarks you will easily recognize (things which will stay the same, not other vehicles near it which might move away), then as you walk away, look back at your car and imagine the route to get back to it from further and further away. [119 words/total 1897]

It's easier to remember something when you are in the same place as you first thought of it, so if you find you've forgotten why you've come upstairs or into another room, instead of actually walking back to the original place, you can close your eyes and imagine you're back where you started. Look around in your mind's eye for what you were planning to do when you were standing in that place. [73 words/total 1970]

Remembering facts for an exam
Information you need for a task which you put immediately into practice is easier to remember than facts for a future exam which have no immediate relevance. For this, you need to create something memorable for your brain to hold on to. [47 words/total 2017]

Organizing your notes into shorter and shorter phrases can be very helpful – the thought you put into editing them ensures that you're understanding the information as well as building memory through repetition. If you can make your notes into a list of keywords, see if you can make the words into an acrostic – a memorable phrase where the first letter of each word is the same as one of the words in your list. "My

Very Easy Method Just Speeds Up Naming (Planets)" gives you the order of the planets in our solar system – Mercury, Venus, Earth, Mars, Jupiter, Saturn, Uranus, Neptune, (Pluto). Alternatively, make up a story which links the original words or the substitute words from your acrostic. If in doubt, try to put words or objects in any sort of order (numerical, size, alphabetical) or pattern. [139 words/total 2156]

Our brains remember the words to songs relatively easily and for quite a long time (people with dementia can often sing along to songs from their younger years). This seems to be to do with the tune and the use of rhyming words, but also because we often hear or sing songs over and over again. Repetition definitely helps memory. And advertisers clearly think that jingles are worth spending money on. Consider making up little songs, rhymes, jingles or dramatic slogans with the facts you want to remember. You probably already know how to remember the number of days in a month from the rhyme:

30 days have September, April, June and November.
All the rest have 31, except February alone
which has but 28 days clear, and 29 in each leap year.

[133 words/total 2289]

Also, try linking facts with movements – like the actors' trick of remembering lines more easily by adding gestures and movement to things they're saying. Even just walking up and down as you learn words can help the process. [38 words/ total 2327]

Pegging

Any book about memory will suggest pegging systems. This is where you have a basic structure which you know (or memorize) like the numbers zero to nine and associated words and then you make a mental link between this and the words or ideas you want to remember. [48 words/2376]

A classic pegging system is based on the children's nursery rhyme which begins, *"One, two, buckle my shoe; three, four, open the door".* You start by learning the numbers zero to nine, each linked to an object which is easy to visualize and rhymes with the number:

Zero – hero; one – bun; two – shoe; three – tree; four – door; five – hive; six – sticks; seven – heaven; eight – gate; nine – vine; ten – hen. [69 words/total 2445]

Then add your words to the numbers by making unusual links between them and your list – maybe start with a shopping list to practise. [24 words/total 2469]

Memory palace – loci system

A "memory palace" or "memory walk" is similar to the pegging system. It is a basic structure to which you add visualizations of things you want to remember. (It was originally called the loci system – "loci" means "places".) You start by itemizing and learning in order a list of 10 things in a room you know well or on a walk you do often, e.g. large tree, road crossing, car park, baker's, Indian restaurant, water fountain, etc. As you get good at using it, you can add additional "rooms" or extend your walk. [97 words/total 2566]

This chapter is just an introduction to the subject of memory and how to work with it. If you want to know more about any of these methods, you can look them up in books or online for deeper learning. Some of these ideas may seem cumbersome or complicated – why not just remember the thing itself? But that's like saying, "Don't give me a tray for these drinks, it's just one more thing to carry". [75 words/total 2641]

Metaphor

One last thing. Are you one of the people who sabotages their attempts to remember by saying something like "I've got a memory like a sieve"? If so, please change your metaphor and say instead, "I'm working on my skills so I can have a memory like an elephant", or "My brain's like a memory bank". Positive thinking can be a very powerful tool. [65 words/total 2706]

ARTICLE

You are recommended to use this article to look for specific words using patterns such as super-reading or zigzag (see p.71). You can also use it to try out other speed reading techniques. Word counts are given.

What Is Reading For?

It is clear that the purpose of reading is to transfer information and ideas between people who are separated by space or time. Obtaining knowledge and wisdom and staying informed are clearly important aspects of reading, and at a deeper level reading enriches the human experience.

Consider the following ways in which reading enriches our lives. [60 words]

Cognitive development

Reading enhances cognitive functions such as comprehension, critical thinking and problem-solving. It stimulates the brain, fostering mental agility and creativity. According to research, regular reading improves brain connectivity, increases vocabulary and comprehension and leads to higher levels of understanding and empathy. [43 words/total 103]

Empathy and perspective

Reading allows individuals to experience lives, cultures and perspectives different from their own. Through fiction and non-fiction, readers can better understand others' emotions and experiences, enhancing empathy and emotional intelligence. This ability to step into someone else's shoes encourages compassion and social unity. [46 words/total 149]

Personal growth and self-reflection

Reading can be a journey of self-discovery. By engaging with diverse ideas and philosophies, individuals can reflect on their values, beliefs and goals. This introspective aspect of reading often leads to personal growth, helping readers navigate their lives with greater wisdom and insight. [47 words/total 196]

Cultural and historical awareness

Through reading, people gain insights into different cultures, historical events and societal structures. This broadens your horizons and builds a more informed and culturally sensitive worldview, promoting tolerance and appreciation for diversity. [36 words/total 232]

Mental escape and relaxation

Reading offers a form of escape from daily stress and reality. Immersing yourself in a good book can provide relaxation and mental rejuvenation, which are essential for reducing stress and maintaining overall well-being. [37 words/total 269]

Philosophical and spiritual texts

These explore fundamental questions about existence, truth, values, knowledge, reason, consciousness and language. Engaging with these ideas allows you to develop your own perspective, think better, gain knowledge and wisdom, and contribute to a shared quest for understanding and meaning. [44 words/total 313]

Moral and ethical clarity

Reading literature and ethical texts helps individuals explore and refine their moral and ethical understanding. Through the dilemmas faced by characters and the arguments presented by authors, readers gain clarity about their own values and the principles behind their actions and beliefs. [46 words/total 359]

Knowledge

In pursuit of knowledge, reading is a fundamental means of seeking and expanding understanding. Whether through scientific texts, historical documents or investigative journalism, reading allows individuals to explore facts, uncover evidence and build an informed understanding of reality. Critical reading skills (such as being able to analyze texts) enable readers to distinguish between trustworthy sources and misinformation (like "fake news"). [61 words/total 420]

Wisdom vs knowledge

Wisdom and knowledge, though often intertwined, are fundamentally different. Knowledge refers to the collection of facts, information and skills acquired through experience or education. It is specific, often measurable, and can change as new discoveries are made – we no longer believe, for example, that the Sun revolves around the Earth. In contrast, wisdom involves lessons and principles that stay constant across different contexts and eras. Wisdom is the common-sense application of knowledge and experience that empowers individuals to navigate life's complexities with foresight and care. Wisdom is often expressed through aphorisms, such as "Prevention is better than cure", which have been relevant for thousands of years. Knowledge can become outdated or refined, whereas wisdom retains its relevance, offering us guidance through the ages. [126 words/total 546]

In essence, reading is a vital tool in the lifelong journey toward knowledge and wisdom. It enriches the mind, sharpens critical thinking and decision-making, fosters empathy and encourages reflection. Engaging with texts through the lens of wisdom and knowledge helps us evaluate and choose better-quality reading sources, ensuring that the information and insights we gain are relevant and lasting. Reading nurtures a lifelong love for learning, expands the mind and connects us to the vast tapestry of human experience. It provides knowledge, solace, adventure, fun and introspection. Beyond transmitting information, reading serves as a cornerstone of personal, transpersonal, spiritual and intellectual fulfilment, leading to an appreciation of the greater concept of wisdom. [187 words/total 733]

QUIZ Two

How quickly can you find – or remember – the answers to these questions about this book? (Maximum 12 points for all correct answers. Answers on p.169)

1. Which technique would you use to ...
    a) get an idea of what the text is about before you read it?
    b) have a clear idea of what you want to get from your reading?
    c) look through the whole text to see if you've missed something?

2. Which of these patterns can you use for speeding up your eyes and your brain?
    a) super-reading b) underlining c) zigzag

3. How many points do we suggest you look for ...
    a) ... in a 20-minute session?
    b) ... in a 75-minute session with 4 texts?

4. When reading, your eyes move in small jumps called ... what?

5. What is a pacer?

6. What is your schema?

7. Who first popularized mindmapping?

8. What is the best kind of lighting for reading?

9. How many times is the word "wisdom" used on pages 141-4?

SPEED TEST – how fast are you reading?

Check your reading speed

If you are interested in finding out your reading speed in wpm (words per minute), do this 3-minute test before and after reading this book.

Note: We recommend you use 2 articles from this book for the before and after tests. If you have already read them, or if you want to check your reading speed again in the future, use any text you haven't read, preferably with uninterrupted text without too many diagrams or images, etc.

3-minute test

Use the article about "How Your Eyes Work" (p.32) which gives word counts after every paragraph.

- Set your timer for 3 minutes and read at your normal speed in your normal way with comprehension (i.e. make sure you understand what you are reading).
- After 3 minutes, stop – and mark your stopping place.
- How well did you understand the text? Grade yourself on a scale of 1–10 (10 = perfectly).
- Count how many words you've read.

- Divide the number of words you've read by 3 to give your reading speed in wpm.

After working with the techniques in this book ...

... do the same 3-minute test with the article "How to Remember" (p.128), which also gives word counts.

Use any techniques you have learned in the book which you think will help you read faster and at your "best comprehension speed" (i.e. as fast as you can while still understanding what you're reading).

Note: Speed is only one aspect of speed reading. As well as comparing your reading speed, compare your level of comprehension and the number of techniques and strategies you use now that help you read more efficiently and effectively.

WHAT IS A GOOD READING SPEED?

150-250 wpm is the average reading speed for adults. 300-500 wpm is a good pace for sequential reading.

Speeds in excess of 1000 wpm are quite common when skimming/scanning very quickly through a text to get a general understanding or when looking for specific information.

However, remember that reading speed can vary tremendously (even for one person), depending on the material and the purpose.

Things That Can Slow Down Your Reading – and what to do about them

If you have already worked through the techniques in this book, you may well find that these things are no longer slowing you down, so only read this if you need to:

- **Regression**
- **Subvocalizing**
- **Being an "auditory" reader**
- **Small vocabulary**
- **Reading - one - word - at - a - time** (see "Read in Meaningful Chunks", p.25)

Regression

Regression means going back and reading something you've already read, usually because your brain's switched off and you haven't understood or can't remember what you just read. Sometimes it just becomes a habit. It obviously slows you down because:

- you're reading something twice rather than once
- going back breaks the flow of the meaning of the text so your brain has to work harder to get back into the meaning (so going back to understand better actually stops you from understanding better).

How to break the habit

- Realize that you're doing it, notice if it happens (being aware of what's going on is a first step to changing).
- Use a piece of blank paper or card as a pacer (p.79). Make sure it's the length of the line you're reading, place it above the top line of the page, and as you read each line, bring the card down to cover that line, so your eyes get used to looking forward rather than back.

Also, use the following techniques until they become better habits. Before you start reading:

- **Get into a good state** to increase your concentration (p.61).
- **Open your peripheral vision** to soften your gaze so your eyes take in more information with each fixation (p.34).
- **Speed up** your eyes and your brain so that you're reading faster (p.68)
- Have a clear **purpose** so you know what you're looking for (p.16).

While you're reading:

- Take fewer fixations as you read (p.59) - or use speed reading patterns such as super-reading or zigzag (p.71) to search for hotspots (p.44) of useful information.

When is going back (regression) OK?

If you've been using a pattern (p.71) and you realize you've passed, or are in the middle of, a hotspot of information you need, it's OK to go back to where that information starts and read more slowly. Sometimes you may also need to go back to understand something earlier in order to understand current information (but don't let this become a habit).

Subvocalizing

Subvocalizing means saying the words to yourself in your head as you read (**vocalizing** means saying the words and actually moving your lips).

Most of us do it sometimes, and it can be useful for understanding a text whose meaning is difficult or which is written in a complicated way. Some people need to subvocalize in order to understand what they're reading. (These are usually people who prefer to take in information by listening rather than reading.)

Subvocalizing will slow you down to about 200-250 words per minute – the maximum speed at which most people speak and the average speed of a reasonably good reader.

You may not subvocalize when speed reading

As you start using speed reading techniques, you may well find that subvocalizing stops or lessens because you can't speak quickly enough to keep up with your brain and because you're looking at much larger blocks of text (rather than sequential phrases).

When we're skimming and scanning through a text very fast, we often use the "voice in our head" to talk to ourselves about the material we're looking at, like this: "Graph showing highest temperatures; same idea; nothing, nothing; I know that; explanation – got it; examples; oh – new thing" (at this point we slow down and possibly take notes before speeding up again).

If you want to subvocalize less ...

... then when you're reading sequentially, only say to yourself the meaning-bearing words rather than all the words (p.46) – that way you'll be able to say more words and read more quickly.

While you're skimming through text for information as fast as you can, try:

- closing your lips and putting your tongue on the roof of your mouth
- chewing gum

Being an "auditory" reader

There are basically 3 types of learners: visual (they like to see things), auditory (they like to hear things) and kinaesthetic (they like to move around and do things). Most people have a preference for one or two of these, and partly it depends what they're learning, but if someone has a very strong preference for auditory learning, they sometimes need to say words to themselves (subvocalize) in order to understand what they're reading. They often need to replay in their heads things they have heard or learned. This can slow them down as they take in information. However, this led many of the auditory learners we know to have a stronger memory of what they've read – and they have to do less work afterwards to remember the information. They can still benefit from all the speed reading techniques which are not based on simply reading faster.

Small vocabulary

This isn't really a reading problem – but having a small vocabulary can slow you down. Reading more and understanding the meaning of words from the context is an easy way to grow your vocabulary.

Your **passive vocabulary** is the words you understand when you hear or see them. Your **active vocabulary** is the words you can use when you're speaking or writing. For reading you only need passive vocabulary (which for most people is much bigger than their active vocabulary).

You can grow your passive vocabulary by **listening to audiobooks, texts or lectures** in situations where you aren't able to read (e.g. when driving).

Jargon is words that mean something specific in a particular subject area, for example, many medical words are used in everyday conversation. Speed reading jargon includes words like *fixations, saccades, skimming, scanning,* etc.

If you need to learn jargon words for any subject:

- Read a book for beginners on the subject which will almost certainly explain jargon as you learn the concepts.
- As you progress, look up jargon in specialist glossaries, either in books or on websites; some apps and computer programs allow you to click on words for an explanation if you need it immediately.

Reassuringly, the more you read, the more your vocabulary will grow.

Reading - one - word - at - a - time

See "Read in Meaningful Chunks" (p.25). This explains in detail how to address this question.

Difficult Texts

Speed reading is always easier and quicker than conventional reading, but sometimes you'll find it harder to find the information you're looking for, either because of textual difficulties or because of your own knowledge.

What makes a text difficult to read?

- physical factors such as a small typeface, muddled layout or thin paper
- a lack of navigational aids such as a contents list, index, good headings or summaries
- some texts are just badly written – the information isn't presented clearly and logically, or the writing style can be tortuous, ambiguous or distracting
- long, huge documents can initially seem daunting (but see p.125).
- lots of vocabulary or jargon that you don't know.

You can fix some of these things. If you can access the text digitally, you can change the font size, use search, look up jargon, etc. Sometimes you can use a different text or read a summary, synopsis or someone else's notes to get an overview. Or maybe you can ask someone for help. But sometimes there's nothing you can do about it and you just have to do your best. It's not a reading or a speed reading problem – it's a problem anyone will have with this text.

Schema

Your schema is everything you know – which builds with age and experience. Your schema is different from anyone else's, so some texts are harder for some people to read than others.

The more you know about the subject or similar subjects, the easier it is to understand the text. The more you know about reading, how to learn and speed reading techniques, the easier it is to identify the information you need. Additionally, your schema helps you predict and fill in missing information, which can increase reading speed.

Unconscious and critical bias

A bias is a tendency to accept one idea over another, and it can affect how we interpret texts. We all have biases, which are shaped by our schema, but often we are unaware of them. Bias is linked to prejudice, i.e. pre-judging a text, often without clearly taking into account actual information.

"Confirmation bias" is a tendency to believe a writer who supports the views we already have and can lead us to avoid or dismiss texts, authors or ideas which we do not already agree with. "Anchoring bias" happens when we fixate on the first information we read and judge subsequent information negatively as a result. "Hindsight bias" is when we believe that past events were "obviously going to happen" – when really they could not have been reliably predicted at the time – leading us to oversimplify complex situations.

The more we are aware of our biases, the easier it is to keep an open mind when reading new material.

SUSPENSION OF DISBELIEF

If you disagree with the writer's point of view, you will probably read it more slowly than if you agree with them. Part of your brain will be thinking about counter-arguments as you read, so even if the author addresses those points further along, you can't get that time back. We recommend reading "as if you agree with the author" – what you might call "a willing suspension of disbelief", an attitude most people are happy to adopt at the cinema, for example. This will help you take in the information more quickly and with an open mind. Evaluate the information, either negatively or positively, at the end once you have all the facts.

Physical Factors

Optimizing certain physical factors can significantly enhance your reading and speed reading skills and overall comprehension.

- **Position of the text or device:** Positioning your text or device at a 45-degree angle (or an angle between 30 and 60 degrees to suit you) can reduce strain on the eyes and neck, which can result in increased reading speeds. Sitting back from the text gives you a wider view and allows you to take in more text at one time.
- **Noise:** A quiet environment enhances concentration. Organize your reading space to minimize distractions, or use noise cancelling headsets or earplugs. Whether or not you have music playing is a personal choice – people are different. If you do play music, preferably choose instrumental or classical music, such as Baroque, which is relaxing yet stimulating. Very loud music or songs with lyrics can be distracting and get in the way of comprehension.
- **Lighting:** Studies show that good lighting can reduce visual fatigue and improve cognitive performance. Natural daylight is ideal, but for evening reading use a combination of ambient light (in the room) and focused task lighting, such as a desk lamp.

Avoid fluorescent lights, which can be harsh and strain your eyes.

- **Monitor position:** Make sure your computer monitor is at eye level. This supports better posture and enhances productivity. Ergonomic research (the study of people's efficiency in their work environment) shows that a properly positioned monitor can increase productivity by up to 30%. When using a laptop or tablet, take regular breaks to avoid neck strain from looking down at the screen.
- **Screen glare:** Reducing glare on screens can help prevent eye strain.
- **Water:** Have a glass of water to hand and drink regularly to keep your brain hydrated.
- **Working environment:** Keep your surroundings comfortable and as free from clutter as possible. Prime yourself and boost your motivation by creating a positive, supportive environment, surrounding yourself with inspiring artwork, plants, personal mementoes and easily accessible books and texts.

Note: Studies suggest that the more books you have around, the more intelligent and knowledgeable you will be. A 2018 study by researchers from the Australian National University and the University of Nevada found that people who grew up in homes with a large number of books showed higher literacy skills in adulthood.

AI For Speed Reading

People are using AI (artificial intelligence) in more and more ways, and it can help you achieve many of the same (or similar) results as some speed reading techniques. If you have already changed your mindset from "How much have I read?" to "How much usable information have I got?", then using AI can speed up this process, particularly for:

- summarizing or getting the main points from texts (especially useful for large texts)
- finding information without having to first identify the texts
- finding answers to specific questions (e.g. how to do something)
- identifying and highlighting specific information
- comparing different texts, as with syntopic reading, by generating a combined understanding of the topic using extracts or summaries from multiple sources
- getting an introduction to a new subject
- producing notes
- writing any findings in the form you need (presentation, report, etc.)

In addition, AI can:

- explain words, jargon and concepts
- translate foreign languages in real time
- produce quizzes, tests and comprehension questions (to help you learn speed reading – or anything else)
- answer specific questions about the text, helping you to understand complex sections without rereading them – particularly useful for academic or technical materials
- generate visual aids like mindmaps, tables or infographics based on the content, helping you to visualize the structure and key points of a text, and enhancing memory retention
- provide real-time feedback and error correction for your notes, acting as an instantaneous feedback mechanism or a coach, highlighting any discrepancies or errors in your understanding, ensuring consistent improvement and accuracy in comprehension
- develop personalized reading plans, suggesting materials that match your interests and challenge your reading speed and comprehension skills
- enhance your focus and state with AI-driven meditation or focus apps to help you get into the optimal mental state for speed reading, reducing distractions and improving concentration
- act as an ever-available discussion partner, helping to reinforce key points, challenge your interpretations and biases, and explore different perspectives

Prompt engineering

To get the most useful information from AI, you need to learn how to use it most effectively: how to ask it the right questions, giving clear, specific prompts which are brief and avoid ambiguity. You also need to evaluate the results you receive each time and think about how you might improve your prompts for next time.

AI is going to get more and more efficient, so you'll need to keep up as it changes. Make sure you're using the right AI tools for the task and that you understand how each tool works and how to use it. Tools could include: AI summarization tools, text-to-speech software or apps that highlight key concepts and ideas in a text.

- **Try out different prompt styles:** direct questions, open-ended prompts or more creative and abstract requests.
- **Use context:** say what you're going to use the information for.

However, even at a basic level, you still have to read and think critically about what AI produces: check that it hasn't made mistakes, that it has fulfilled your purpose (make sure you set a purpose), that it has prioritized the right things and that it hasn't missed anything.

We say that speed reading puts you in charge of information so that you are using the text, rather than the text using you. AI is a useful tool, but make sure that you are in control of anything that AI produces.

Q&A

These are the questions we've been asked most frequently – and our answers.

Will speed reading help me concentrate better?

Absolutely. Having a clear purpose means you know what you're looking for and stops you from getting sidetracked. Having a strict time limit motivates you to keep reading to find the information quickly – and 20 minutes doesn't seem like too much of a challenge when you're getting started. Getting into a good state every time you do a reading task also builds up the habit of being focused and in control.

Does speed reading affect comprehension?

Speed reading can sometimes compromise comprehension, especially if the focus is solely on speed. On the other hand, taking in more information more quickly can make it easier to understand a text. Effective speed reading requires a balance between pace and understanding. Techniques like previewing, skimming and scanning give you the gist of the text, after which other techniques such as purpose, syntopic processing and rapid reading help you get a deeper understanding of complex subjects.

Does speed reading help people with dyslexia?

We are experts in speed reading, not dyslexia, but our experience is that our approach to speed reading can be very effective for individuals with dyslexia. Many of the techniques are more in tune with the dyslexic way of thinking than traditional strategies commonly used to teach children to read. We suggest you start using the techniques and prove it for yourself.

What are the biggest barriers to speed reading?

In our experience, the biggest challenges are perfectionism and your "inner critic". Wanting "everything" from a text from a first read is bound to slow anyone down - as well as being a very inefficient way of getting information. Focus on your purpose (p.16) to decide what you actually want or need. What you're aiming for is "enough".

If the voice inside your head is giving you negative messages, change them to something positive: "I just need a bit of practice to do this well"; "This is really going to save me a lot of time. Look at how much I've improved already."

I've tried speed reading but I don't think I'm very good at it. What can I do?

In the early days people can be slowed down because they're thinking too much about the process, rather than focusing on the content (the text, their purpose and finding the information they need). As soon as you know what you're doing and focus on the reading, you can speed up. Also people who are "testing the system" tend not to do so well. Put the techniques into practice with texts you need to read and focus on your reading – and see how quickly you improve.

At what age can people start speed reading?

We usually recommend that young people start learning speed reading techniques shortly before they go to secondary school – or definitely before they start at college or university. However, we have had students as young as 8 and as old as 76 on our courses.

What can I do with my younger children to help them get ready for speed reading?

Once young children have learned how to decipher and write letters and words, you can show them how to look ahead along the line to make sense of a phrase before they read it aloud to you (p.28). Play reading games with them, for example with little children, "This word says 'dinosaur'. Can you find the same word 'dinosaur' somewhere else on the page?" Give older children a list of words you know are in the index of a factual book and challenge them to see how quickly they can find those words on the different pages of the book. (You could show them the different patterns for looking down a page (p.71). If they're keen you can try "Just Read Faster" (p.65). However, the biggest predictor of someone becoming a good reader is how much they were read to as a small child. It's not how much they themselves read – "being read to" means that the child associates feelings of pleasure and happiness with reading, which they're then more likely to want to do themselves. Taking time to sit down and read with your children is a great investment in their future. Have books around for them to find, and they'll know reading is important to you if they see you enjoying it.

Do I really need a purpose for reading?

Many people (including us) think that having a purpose is one of the most important speed reading techniques (and it doesn't even involve reading faster). After all, you know how chaotic meetings can be if they don't have an agenda. Most books just say "Make sure you have a purpose for reading" but they don't explain what that means. We've given as much explanation as possible (p.16), but once you've understood what it means, you can do it very quickly, usually as you preview your text.

If it's taking longer than that to set a purpose, make sure you're not trying to find the 6 points in your purpose while you're setting it. Setting your purpose is simply deciding on what your aim is for reading this text (e.g. "find 6 points for ..."), not completing that aim. You will find those 6 things while you're reading in a subsequent 20-minute session (p.90).

Will I still enjoy reading for pleasure?

Absolutely. Our approach to speed reading is to give you techniques which allow you to read at a speed appropriate to your wants and needs - you're in control. You can speed up to get factual information quickly and slow down when you're reading for pleasure (if that's what gives you pleasure).

What if I want all the details?

You probably don't need **all** the details, so decide what details you want about which things (and what you want to do with them). Then have a work session for a maximum of 20 minutes (p.90) to look for them. If you still feel you may have missed some important details, then rapid read (p.98) to check - and look at p.93 to deal with the feeling of having missed something. The more you put the techniques into practice, the more you will come to trust in your abilities. The more you trust yourself and the system, the more proficient you will become at speed reading.

Do you have one tip for reluctant readers?

Read more. Reading is one of the best ways to build your knowledge and vocabulary. The brain gets good at what it's used to, so reading gets easier the more you do it. Read anything that appeals to you - this will encourage you to keep reading more. Speed reading techniques allow you to read more, quicker.

What techniques will help me most?

Preview (p.10), Purpose (p.16) and State (p.61).

Is it worth my time to learn to speed read?

We definitely think so. Here are all the ways speed
reading saves us time:

- reading quicker – every text
- previewing – finding out that texts aren't worth
  reading (instead of reading something through and
  then deciding it was a waste of time); and deciding
  how much of a text is worth reading and how much
  information it might contain
- setting a clear purpose so we don't waste time
- sticking to the 80/20 rule – doing things as well as
  necessary and getting rid of the feeling of needing to
  do everything perfectly. (We need to do some things
  perfectly – but not many)
- working in 20-minute blocks – it's amazing how much
  more we get done if we limit ourselves to 20 minutes
- getting in a good state before we start so that we can
  concentrate
- applying lots of these ideas to things other than speed
  reading!

We really wish we'd known all of this much earlier in life
– and definitely before going to university.

But is this "proper" reading?

If by "proper" you mean slow conventional reading, then no. But it's the approach most really good readers use, whether they've been taught speed reading or worked out some of these techniques for themselves.

Compare conventional with speed reading to see how far you've come:

Conventional reading	Speed reading
Read all texts in the same way	Have a variety of techniques you can use
Attention can wander	Stay focused
Usually forget 90% within 48 hours	Remember as much as you need for as long as you need
Takes a long time to get information	Get the information you need quickly
The writer determines how you get information (whether you need it or not)	You're in control of getting the information that is relevant to you
The idea is that reading slowly is enough to make you an expert	You have techniques to build your expertise quickly and easily

Answers

How Eyes Work: Predictability (p.42)

2. UPPER: Notice how relatively easy it is to read a text where you can only see the tops of letters.
LOWER: It can be more difficult to understand if you can only see the bottoms of letters.

3. a. to (doing something). b. saves nine. c. birthday. d. on the other (+ something negative). e. success. f. death. g. bigger. h. remember. i. know. j. wild

Quiz One (p.80)

1. Parkinson's law (p.82). 2. Priming (p.52). 3. When you need to read hotspots of key information, or details. Big picture before details (p.15). 4. Thin slicing (p.70). 5. Pareto principle (or 80/20 rule) (p.88). 6. Difference (for new learning). Sameness and difference (p.96)

Quiz Two (p.145)

1a. preview. 1b. set a purpose. 1c. rapid reading. 2. all of them. 3a. 6. 3b. 11. 4. saccades. 5. something you use to set the pace for your reading, e.g. your finger or a capped pen. 6. the sum of the personal knowledge held in one's brain. 7. Tony Buzan. 8. "Natural daylight is ideal" (p.157). 9. 12.

Congratulations if you got all 12 answers correct – and especially for working out where to find the information.

Mindmap Of
Speed Reading Faster

In "Take Notes" (p.83), we suggested you do an overview mindmap of this book. Opposite is our mindmap for you to compare. Look through it and check back in the book if there's anything you don't understand.

MINDMAP OF *SPEED READING FASTER*

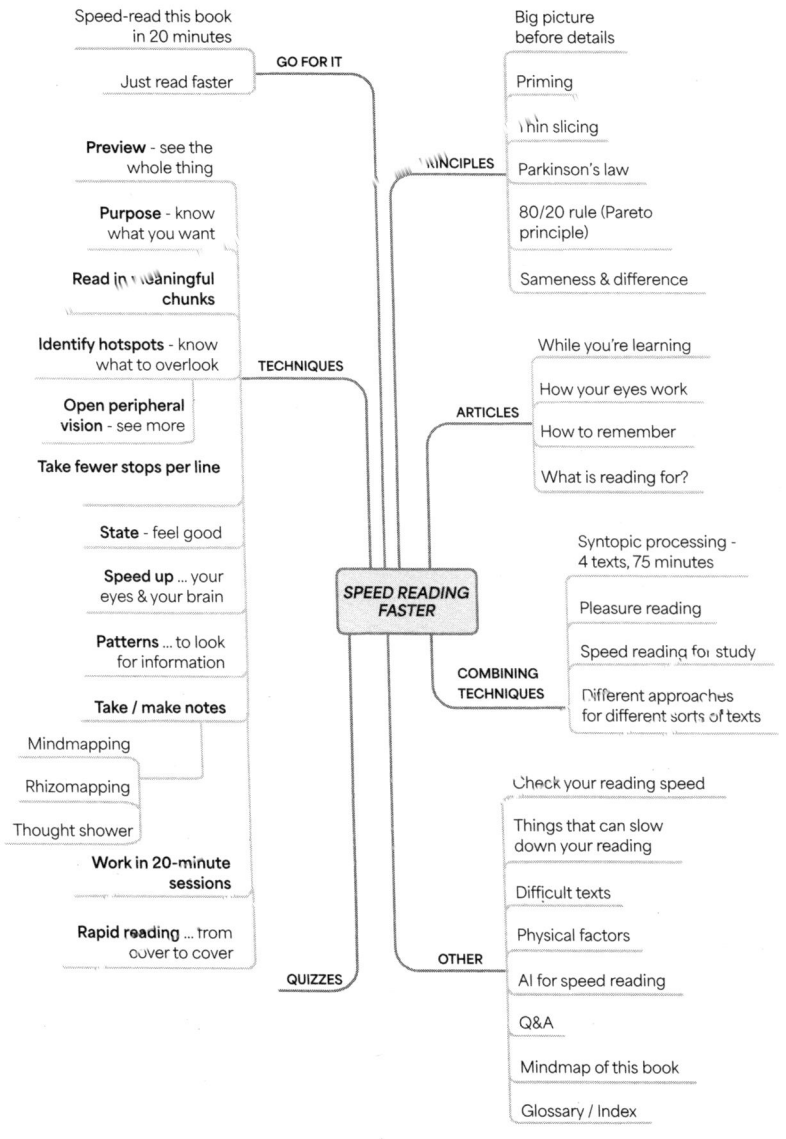

Speed-read this book in 20 minutes

Just read faster

GO FOR IT

Big picture before details

Priming

Thin slicing

Parkinson's law

80/20 rule (Pareto principle)

Sameness & difference

PRINCIPLES

Preview - see the whole thing

Purpose - know what you want

Read in meaningful **chunks**

Identify hotspots - know what to overlook

Open peripheral vision - see more

Take fewer stops per line

TECHNIQUES

While you're learning

How your eyes work

How to remember

What is reading for?

ARTICLES

State - feel good

Speed up ... your eyes & your brain

Patterns ... to look for information

Take / make notes

Mindmapping

Rhizomapping

Thought shower

Work in 20-minute sessions

Rapid reading ... from cover to cover

SPEED READING FASTER

Syntopic processing - 4 texts, 75 minutes

Pleasure reading

Speed reading for study

Different approaches for different sorts of texts

COMBINING TECHNIQUES

Check your reading speed

Things that can slow down your reading

Difficult texts

Physical factors

AI for speed reading

Q&A

Mindmap of this book

Glossary / Index

OTHER

QUIZZES

GLOSSARY / INDEX

Looking through the glossary can be a helpful way to review the many aspects of speed reading from a different perspective. If there's anything you're not sure of, you can easily look it up.

About The Authors

Jan Cisek has been teaching speed reading for over 25 years, helping thousands worldwide enhance their reading and learning skills. He integrates Accelerated Learning, NLP, and systems thinking, making learning efficient, effective and creative as well as fun. Jan has presented at numerous conferences on speed reading and accelerated learning. He is also an environmental psychologist, exploring the impact of the environment on learning. He co-authored *Spd Rdng - The Speed Reading Bible* with Susan Norman, which encapsulates their combined expertise in speed reading, accelerated learning and personal development. *Speed Reading Faster* is his second book on speed reading.

Susan Norman is a world expert in accelerated learning, and started working with Jan in 2000. They've been teaching speed reading together ever since for schools, businesses, banks and local authorities, as well as public courses and one-to-one. She was co-director of the Society of Effective Affective Learning and on the board of the (US) International Alliance for Learning. Susan is the author of more than 50 published books, mostly on learning and teaching English, for Pearson, BBC, Cornelsen and more, and has taught teachers, run courses and given presentations throughout Europe and beyond.

More info: spdrdng.com